GREAT
WEAPONS
OF WORLD
WAR
II

GREAT WEAPONS OF WORLD WAR II

BY JOHN KIRK AND ROBERT YOUNG JR.

WITH AN INTRODUCTION BY BERNARD E. TRAINOR

WALKER AND COMPANY ❋ NEW YORK

Copyright © 1990 by John Kirk and Robert Young Jr.

All rights reserved. No part off this book may be reproduced or
transmitted in any form or by any means, electronic or mechanical,
including photocopying, recording, or by any information storage and
retrieval system, without permission in writing from the Publisher.

First published in the United States of America in 1990
by Walker Publishing Company, Inc.

Published simultaneously in Canada by Thomas Allen & Son
Canada, Limited, Markham, Ontario

Library of Congress Cataloging-in-Publication Data

Kirk, John G.
Great weapons of World War II / by John Kirk and
Robert Young, Jr. ; with an introduction by Bernard E. Trainor.
ISBN 0-8027-1138-3
1. Munitions—History—20th century. 2. World War, 1939–1945–
–Equipment. 3. Armed Forces—Equipment—History—20th century.
I. Young, Robert, 1927–   . II. Title.
UF520.K5   1990
355.8′2′09044—dc20   90-12642

Printed in the United States of America

2 4 6 8 10 9 7 5 3 1

PREFACE

WORLD WAR II, THE MOST MECHANIZED WAR IN HISTORY, WAS FOUGHT with a profusion of complex, formidable weapons which radically affected the course of events in our century. It is nearly impossible to understand the war—to read its history or the memoirs of its participants, or even to watch documentary films about it—without some knowledge of the terrible machines with which it was fought.

One cannot, for example, fully understand the Battle of Britain without knowing something about Spitfires and Messerschmitts. America's strategy in the Pacific is meaningful only in terms of the weapons and techniques of amphibious and carrier warfare. The story of Rommel and Montgomery is largely one of Shermans, PzKw IV's, 25-pounders and "88" 's.

The purpose of this book is to furnish the general reader with a necessary minimum of information about the great weapons of World War II. The text is divided into 80 illustrated sections, each dealing with a particular weapon or class of weapons. The amount of space devoted to various weapons is not, however, in any sort of proportion to their relative importance. Equal space, for example, is given to the atomic bomb and to midget submarines. But there the comparison ends.

The authors are only too well aware that much has been left out. Volumes could be written about each of the weapons mentioned in this book and about all the other important weapons which have not been included because of lack of space. And at that, only lethal weapons are discussed. Such vitally important pieces of equipment as radar, sonar, jeeps, trucks, C-47's, bulldozers and so forth have been omitted categorically, despite the fact that some of them were more important to the outcome of the war than most of the machines of pure destruction. The authors can only acknowledge these omissions and ask for the reader's indulgence.

Even though it attempts to treat a technical subject in as non-technical a way as possible, GREAT WEAPONS could never have been prepared without the invaluable assistance of a number of military experts both in and out of the armed services. Profoundest thanks is due to Mr. Hanson W. Baldwin, military commentator for *The New York Times,* for his encouragement, comments and advice; to LCDR Arnold Lott, USN Ret., of the United States Naval Institute, for his comments on the naval sections of the manuscript; to the staff of the U.S. Air Force Historical Section for their comments on "Aircraft"; to Miss Edith Midgette, Chief of the Magazine and Book Section, and Mr. Robert W. Harvey, Chief of the Photo Branch, Office of the Assistant Secretary of Defense, for their many kindnesses and services; and to Mrs. Sarah F. Raddin, Director of the Cranford, N.J., Public Library for her help in gathering research material.

A special debt of gratitude is due Col. G. B. Jarrett, USAR, Ret., Director of the Ordnance Museum at the Aberdeen Proving Ground in Maryland, for his help in preparing the "land weapons" sections (nearly 50 per cent) of GREAT WEAPONS. Col. Jarrett probably knows more about modern military weapons than any living man and a visit to his staggering collection of historic arms is a must for anyone interested in the hardware of war. Virtually everything is there, from General Pershing's Locomobile staff car to "Anzio Annie," from Civil War rifles to Tiger tanks.

Plainly, neither Hanson Baldwin, Col. Jarrett, nor the other expert individuals who so graciously lent their assistance in the preparation of GREAT WEAPONS can be held accountable for any errors of fact or interpretation which may still remain. For these the authors acknowledge sole responsibility.

JOHN KIRK
ROBERT YOUNG, JR.

CONTENTS

GREAT WEAPONS OF WORLD WAR II

INTRODUCTION

THE SECOND WORLD WAR WAS FOUGHT WITH WEAPONS MORE AKIN TO those of the previous great war than those of today's armed forces. Bombs and artillery were chemically based, tanks and aircraft were powered by reciprocating engines and steam propelled warships. It was only in the waning days of the war that the nature of war was changed with the advent of nuclear power, jet propulsion, and long range missilery. These developments reached a point where war on the grand scale today is suicidal and largely unthinkable. For lesser wars, soldiers now wear kevlar protective armor, move by helicopter, turn night into day with ambient light enhancing goggles, and direct laser beams at their targets. It is no wonder soldiers of the forties identify more with the weapons their uncles fought with in 1917 than they do with those of their sons and grandchildren.

That is not to say that the 1939–45 war was bereft of sophisticated weapons or innovative means of employing them. World War II was not a replay of 1914–18, wherein infantry measured gains in yards against artillery barrages and interlocking bands of machine gun fire. On the contrary, it was a war of fire and maneuver made possible by the technical weapons of the machine age. The tank dominated the ground war in Europe, warships decided battles in the Pacific, and the airplane was lord of battle over both land and sea.

World War II also witnessed a new feature in warfare, the combined arms battle. The Germans were the first to master this technique. They integrated Stuka divebombing raids with artillery fire and armored infantry attacks to penetrate the defenses of the Poles and later the Anglo-French armies. The allies were quick to learn the lesson and they too integrated all arms into their tactics. Soon they bettered their foes at the technique.

The Soviets became masters of the set-piece combined arms battle, using the T-34 tank and massive artillery as its centerpiece in the east. On the western front General George Patton's American Third Army excelled in the mobile version of the combined arms battle. Small combat commands made up of armor, infantry, artillery, and engineers supported by P-51s and P-47s spearheaded drives across France into Germany while American and British B-17 "Flying Fortresses" and Blenheim bombers made a shambles of German installations and lines of communications in the rear.

In the Pacific, amphibious forces backed by aircraft carrier battle groups leapfrogged across the Pacific and relentlessly battered the Japanese with a combination of land, sea, and air attack. The German dive bombing technique, so terrifying to defenders at the outset of the war, was refined by U.S. Marine close air support using the venerable gull-winged Corsair. All the while the Japanese home islands were being pummeled by long-range B-29 bombers and strangled by scores of submarines until two atomic bombs wrote finis to the war and ushered in the nuclear age.

Innovative tactics by both sides marked the war and differed according to the theatre of war as did the relative importance of specific weapons. The war in the Libyan desert was fought differently from that in the jungles of Burma. The gigantic Soviet offenses on the plains of Russia differed markedly from the war of maneuver in the western Pacific. British and American tactics on the continent had their own uniqueness. In truth World War II was not one war, but many separate wars, fought not according to stiff doctrine or dogma, but on the basis of what worked and what didn't. The practitioners of war in the forties were pragmatic men if nothing else. Whether at the squad or army group level theory had little place. The theories of Clausewitiz and Jomini were left to war colleges to debate. On the battlefield what counted was results. Survival depended upon it.

In a chicken- and egg-conundrum, some weapons grew out of a need, while in other instances use was found because of the capability of the weapons themselves. At the infantry level, the 2.36 "bazooka" is a classic example of a weapon that was designed to meet a need, but at the same time opened up new tactical possibilities. Designed as a close-in weapon against tanks, it found greater use on some battlefields as a bunker-busting weapon. The same may be said of operational concepts. The American strategy of seizing Japanese-held islands in the central Pacific was originally designed to provide secure bases for the fleet as it advanced upon Japan. But by war's end its prime purpose was to establish airfields to support strategic bombing attacks against the home islands. It should be remembered that the lives of more bomber crews were saved by the capture of Iwo Jima, which was astride the bombing route to Japan, than were lost in the bloody struggle for the island itself. Paradoxically, Tinion, a Navy target turned out to be the launch point for Enola Gay, the B-29 which dropped the first atomic bomb.

In the development of weapons during the war the most dramatic changes took place in aircraft and in armor. Artillery, small arms, and other weapons improved dramatically over the course of six years of fighting, but none to match the improvement in these two arms. Aircraft at the outset of the war were fragile and of limited range and payload. By the end of the war, the Germans had introduced the first jet fighter, while the United States had perfected the long range strategic bomber. On the ground, the German tanks that rolled over Poland in 1939, were puny compared to the Tiger and T-34 tanks that shot it out against one another in 1945. Each of the combatants contributed its share to the deadly arsenal except Japan. Going into the war the Japanese had what was probably the best fighter plane in the world, the famed Zero, but thereafter Japan failed to develop any significantly new or innovative weaponry. The reason was its weak industrial base. It was forced to depend upon the Bushido spirit of its warriors rather than its industry to fight the west and in this it failed. This points up the fact that the Second World War was an industrial war. The side with the greatest weapons-making capacity was bound to win. In this the German and Japanese coalition was doomed particularly when faced with the industrial capacity of the United States which became the arsenal for its allies.

But the weapons which were used by both sides met the test of battle over the course of the greatest war ever fought, and many of them became classics and antecedants for the weapons of today. The war has now been over for forty five years. The men that flew the planes, sailed the ships, and fired the guns are growing fewer and with them an appreciation for its intensity. But to know the weapons of World War II is to know much of how the war was fought: *Great Weapons of World War II* helps to do so by illustrating the panoply of weaponry used. While comprehensive, it is not exhaustive, for such would be nigh impossible given the infinite variety of weapons used. However, the weapons that counted in the struggle are all included in the text and provides the reader a richer appreciation for the weapons and equipment used during the gigantic world-wide struggle that was World War II.

Bernard E. Trainor
April 1990

AIRCRAFT

AIRPLANES WERE USED AS WEAPONS OF WAR APPROXIMATELY ELEVEN years after the Wright Brothers flew at Kitty Hawk. Within thirty years they had become one of the most potent—some, like Douhet and Seversky, said *the* most potent—means of destruction ever devised.

Technical progress in the development of military aviation during the inter-war and war years was astonishing. The British S.E. 5 fighter of World War I had a top speed of 122 m.p.h.; the Spitfire Mk. I of 1939, 365 m.p.h.; the Messerschmitt 262 of 1945, 540 m.p.h. The German Gotha G5 bomber of World War I carried less than two tons of bombs; the Avro Lancaster Mk. III of 1944 carried up to eleven tons a far greater distance.

Yet for all the havoc they wrought and despite their huge contribution to victory, the aircraft of World War II were far from the ultimate weapons which pre-war proponents of air power had claimed them to be. Strategic bombing did not, by itself, break enemy morale or fatally injure enemy industry. It was not until the advent of nuclear explosives that the airplane seemed to give promise of overshadowing other instruments of war. But even then, the emerging science of military rocketry was preparing the way for the decline of the warplane.

It is entirely possible that by the end of the century aircraft will have only minor importance as lethal weapons. If this is so, they will have held the spotlight of military history for a vastly shorter time than, say, the long bow, the mangonel or the morgenstern. Of all the weapons of World War II, airplanes had perhaps the most sinister glamor. If today we feel a little nostalgic about them, it may in part be because the weapons which have succeeded them are so much less glamorous and so very much more terrible.

The Vickers Supermarine Spitfire

LESS THAN A YEAR AFTER BRITAIN DECLARED WAR UPON GERMANY, SHE stood alone. Poland, Denmark, Belgium, the Netherlands, Norway and France had fallen, and in the spring of 1940, the logical sequel was an invasion of England following hard upon a concentrated air attack designed to wipe out the Royal Air Force.

Revived and regrouped after the Battle of France, the German Air Force made ready to strike across the English Channel from airfields in France and Belgium. In July, 1940, the Battle of Britain impended; and, as Winston Churchill said, "Our fate now depended upon victory in the air."

The important thing to understand about the Battle of Britain is that it was essentially a fighter duel. Viewed in retrospect, bombings of civilian and industrial targets not immediately concerned with maintaining the RAF were of secondary importance. Only by establishing complete air superiority could the *Luftwaffe* hope to guarantee a cross-Channel invasion effort. And the issue of air superiority depended on whether nearly 1,000 Messerchmitt Bf 109's and Bf 110's could drive some 200 Spitfires and 400 Hurricanes from the British skies.

Since the Hawker Hurricane was generally inferior to the Bf 109, the RAF attempted, in so far as possible, to assign this sturdy aircraft the task of destroying German bombers. Top-cover, the fighter-versus-fighter role, fell to the elegant, the never-to-be-forgotten, Vickers Supermarine Spitfire, Marks I and II.

This great fighter had a distinguished pedigree. The creation of a

Showing its famed elliptical wings, a Spitfire Mk.VB of No. 92 Squadron goes into a shallow bank. The "B" wings on this Mk.V mounted two 20mm. cannon and four .303 cal. machine guns.

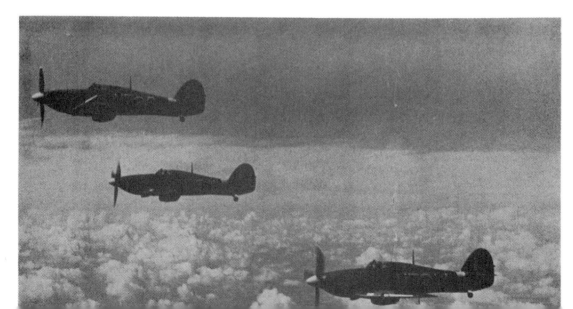

This Seafire IIC, a conversion of the RAF's Spitfire Mk. V, was designed for service on the Royal Navy's aircraft carriers.

The Mk. IX was the most widely produced of all Spitfire variants. Most Mk. IX's used "C" wings which mounted either eight .303 machine guns or two 20mm. cannon and four machine guns or four cannon and four machine guns.

These Hawker Hurricane Mk. IIA's, like the early versions of the Spitfire, carried four .303 cal. machine guns in each wing. Capable of 342 m.p.h. at altitude, the IIA was slower than its Messerschmitt contemporaries.

brilliant designer named Reginald Mitchell, the Spitfire was the evolutionary descendant of a peacetime racer, the S-6B, which in 1931 retired the Schneider Trophy in Britain's favor with a speed of 406.99 m.p.h. The first Spitfire came into being when Mitchell deliberately went beyond the requirements of the 1934 Air Ministry fighter specification to produce a plane which combined the best features of advanced military and racing design concepts. Produced as the Spitfire Mk. I, the aircraft was in service with nineteen RAF squadrons in August, 1940, when the Battle of Britain began. It was, at the time, almost certainly the best operational fighter plane in the world.

What the Spitfires and Hurricanes accomplished that autumn is a story too familiar to need retelling. Even before the end of August, when Goering angrily demanded of a group of his elite pilots what they needed for victory, Adolph Galland, then one of Germany's leading aces, could reply bitterly, "Spitfires, Herr Reichsmarshall."

In the months which followed the Battle of Britain, the improved Messerschmitt Bf 109F gained temporary superiority over the Spitfire Mk. V but lost it again—for good, this time—to the Spitfire Mk. IX.

In all, from Mark I through Mark XXII, the Spitfire underwent some forty major modifications. Spitfires fought in every important theatre of operations and were produced in greater numbers than any other British aircraft.

TECHNICAL NOTES: The Battle of Britain Spitfire Mk. 1A had a 1,030 h.p. Merlin III liquid-cooled engine, a top speed of 365 m.p.h. at 19,000 ft., a range of 575 miles, a span of 37 ft. and an armament of eight .303 cal. machine guns. The Mark IXE (H.F.) had a 1,720 h.p. Merlin 70 engine, a top speed of 416 m.p.h. and an armament of two 20mm. cannon and two .50 cal. machine guns.

The Messerschmitt Bf 109

DESTINED TO BE GERMANY'S STANDARD SINGLE-SEAT FIGHTER FOR MORE than a decade, the Messerschmitt Bf 109 was originated in 1934 as the result of a specification from the German Air Ministry which demanded a monoplane replacement for the budding *Luftwaffe*'s obsolete biplane fighters. Four manufacturers were assigned to produce prototypes; Professor Willy Messerschmitt's design prevailed. The process of testing and modification was begun and continued into 1936, when the first public display of the plane was made during the Olympic Games in Berlin.

Initially, Europe's knowledge of the Bf 109 was derived from hearsay and Nazi press propaganda. Resulting scepticism forced Germany to back up her boasting with a practical display. This took place brilliantly at the 1937 International Flying Meet held in Zurich. Soon after, Hitler seized the opportunity to "field test" the plane by putting it to work in Spain for General Franco. There the Bf 109 proved it deserved first-rank as a fighter.

The long pre-war period of testing and modification resulted, in 1939, in the production of the first of the great war-time Messerschmitts: the Bf 109E. Resistlessly, the Bf 109's and their twin-engined stablemates, the Messerschmitt Bf 110's, swept across Poland, Scandinavia, and the Low Countries. Over France they encountered stiffer opposition from the Moranes and Dewoitines of the Armée de l'Air and from the handful of Hurricanes operating with the British Expeditionary Force. But while the Bf 110 proved inferior to the best French and British fighters, the qualitative supremacy of the Bf 109 was never in doubt.

The last major modification of the Messerschmitt Bf 109 was the G-series. This Bf 109G, captured by the British and marked with their insignia, had a 1,475 h.p. DB605 engine and a top speed of 387 m.p.h.

The standard German fighter during the Battle of Britain was the Messerschmitt Bf 109E.

Following upon their failure as escort fighters, many Messerschmitt Bf 110's after 1942 were equipped with radar and used as night fighters.

One of France's best fighters, the Dewoitine D.520 had a top speed of 329 m.p.h. and an armament of four 7.5mm. machine guns and one 20mm. cannon. D.520's were credited with shooting down 114 enemy planes before the fall of France.

It was only when the Bf 109 encountered the Spitfire in the Battle of Britain that the formidable German fighter finally met its match. The Mark I Spitfire was certainly superior to the E-model Messerschmitt, but the superiority was only marginal. The Spitfire, at medium and low altitudes, was both faster and more maneuverable, but the Messerschmitt had a better rate of climb, a greater diving speed and a higher ceiling.

The improved Messerschmitt Bf 109F, which went into service in January, 1941, was designed to master both the Spitfire Mk. I and whatever successive developments of the Spitfire the British might plan to produce. In this it was successful, but only marginally and only temporarily. For whereas development beyond the "F" modification encountered delays, the Spitfire improved steadily. By the end of 1942, the Messerschmitt had finally lost the race for design supremacy to its old rival.

But from the first to last, the Bf 109 was a very good aircraft and one always to be treated with a maximum of respect. Indeed, the war's highest-scoring aces were, for the most part, Messerschmitt pilots. No Allied airmen even came close to the record of Germany's greatest ace, Major Erich Hartmann of Jagdgeschwader Fifty-two: 352 confirmed victories.

TECHNICAL NOTES: The Messerschmitt Bf 109E had a 1,100 h.p. DB601A liquid-cooled engine, a top speed of 354 m.p.h. at 12,300 ft., a span of over 32 ft. and an armament of two 20mm. cannon and two 7.9mm. machine guns. The Bf 109F-3 had a top speed of 390 m.p.h. at 22,000 ft. and was armed with one 15mm. cannon and two 7.9mm. machine guns.

The Focke-Wulf Fw 190

APPROXIMATELY NINE MONTHS AFTER THE R.A.F. REPELLED THE *Luftwaffe*'s attempt to destroy British air power, Germany put into operation a sleek, wasp-like fighter that was to reign supreme in combat for nearly two years. It was the fabulous Focke-Wulf Fw 190A, which first saw action the summer of 1941.

The result of experiment and development as lengthy and as detailed as that which produced the Messerschmitt Bf 109, the Fw 190 was then the closest answer to perfection in a combat aircraft. Beautifully proportioned, it was a masterpiece of design and construction which took into careful account the problems of production and of maintenance in the field.

There were two major variants of the basic Fw 190 design, and they were, as a matter of fact, radically different. The Fw 190A was powered by a 1,700 h.p. BMW radial engine. The Fw 190D, which went into service in late 1943 had an elongated nose in which was housed a 2,240 h.p. Junkers Jumo in-line engine. It is probably fair to say that the Fw 190D, if not the best fighter of World War II, was at least the peer of the best. But it was the "A" variant which was produced in the greatest quantities and played the more important role.

From the first, the Fw 190A showed itself to be superior to the Spitfire. Its handling was nearly effortless, even at high speeds when it amazed friend and enemy alike by executing aileron turns which would have torn the wings from any other airplane then in use, Allied or Axis.

The Focke-Wulf Fw 190A was markedly superior to any available Allied fighter when it first appeared in combat in the summer of 1941. By early 1942, the Fw 190A accounted for more than half of Germany's monthly single-engine fighter production.

The Focke-Wulf Ta 152 was the final development of the Fw 190D "long nose" series. The Fw 190D's and Ta 152's were the best piston-engine fighters built by Germany.

The Heinkel He 100D was planned as a replacement for the Messerschmitt but never became operational. German propagandists, however, distributed many photographs of the plane (referred to as the He 113) and fooled the Allies into thinking it was one of the **Luftwaffe**'s mainstays.

Reports of the plane's performance produced joy in Berlin, and a mixture of respect and consternation in London. The fighter was, as Hitler and Goering hoped, the replacement for the Messerschmitt Bf 109 that the Battle of Britain showed Germany needed.

This superb fighter did not, however, blossom overnight under the pressure of the demand for a successor to the Bf 109. Rather, the Focke-Wulf Fw 190 was the German Air Ministry's "ace in the hole," ordered developed in 1937 to supplement the Messerschmitt. Once undertaken, development was brought to fruition quickly. Construction of the first of a number of Fw 190 prototypes was initiated the summer of 1938. Flight testing got underway ten months later.

By early 1940, the plane neared the point of mass production. What was then the most advanced prototype was inspected by Goering. Greatly impressed, he told Focke-Wulf design team chief Kurt Tank that he "must turn these new fighters out like so many hot rolls!" This was done, although the number of Fw 190's produced as fighters and fighter-bombers came nowhere near that of the Bf 109.

In June, 1942, the Allies fell heir to a bit of luck. A *Luftwaffe* pilot landed in Britain with his Fw 190A in top-notch condition. British study of the remarkable plane resulted in orders for the building of the Hawker Fury, in which were incorporated numerous features copied directly from the German fighter. Among airmen this was high tribute, justly due a great warplane.

TECHNICAL NOTES: The Focke-Wulf Fw 190A-8 had a 1,700 h.p. BMW 801-2 air-cooled engine, a top speed of 408 m.p.h. at 20,600 ft., a span of 34.5 ft. and an armament of two 13mm. machine guns and four 20mm. cannon. The Fw 190D-9 had a top speed of 426 m.p.h.; the Ta 152C had a top speed of 463 m.p.h.

The Republic P-47 Thunderbolt

THE UNITED STATES FIRST GAINED ACCLAIM FOR ITS FIGHTERS WITH THE debut of the chubby Republic P-47 Thunderbolt in combat over Europe in April, 1943.

Evolved from experience gained in the development of the P-43 Lancer and P-44, the Thunderbolt was at the time the largest and heaviest one-man single-engine fighter ever built. Comparison with the Spitfire and Focke-Wulf was like that of the bee with the mosquito. Upon seeing the P-47, R.A.F. pilots chided their American colleagues, insisting that they could best escape flak and machine gun fire by slipping out of harness and dodging about inside the Thunderbolt's huge fuselage!

Nevertheless, size was no detriment to the Thunderbolt's performance. Like many a fat man who reveals himself light and fast on his feet when necessary, the Thunderbolt delivered the goods.

Between 1943 and 1945, Thunderbolts flew more than 500,000 combat sorties. They lumbered into the air weighing up to a maximum of 17,600 lbs. But once up, Thunderbolts were nimble and telling in combat.

Also, the airplane could take a phenomenal amount of punishment. It became renowned for an ability to absorb battle damage and return home. One Eighth Air Force P-47 flew back to its base in England with nine of its 18 engine cylinders shot out; another, with four feet sheered off its right wing.

The massiveness of the Thunderbolt extended to its offensive arma-

A P-47C Thunderbolt marked with ETO tail stripes and the white cowling of the 78th Fighter Group executes a climbing turn over an English air base.

The Lockheed P-38 was a good high-altitude escort fighter but lacked the maneuverability and performance to put it on an equal footing with the best German interceptors.

Thunderbolts from the P47D-20 series on featured "bubble" cockpit canopies. This P-47D, carrying ten 5-inch HVAR rockets, gives some idea of the Thunderbolt's potential as a fighter-bomber.

ment. Its eight .50 calibre machine guns were estimated to have an impact equivalent to the force of a 6-ton truck striking a wall at thirty miles per hour.

The importance of the P-47 lay in the fact that it was the first Allied fighter able to meet Messerschmitts and Focke-Wulfs on approximately equal terms while at the same time possessing sufficient range to escort the daylight bombers deep into Germany. Of the two previously-used escort fighters, the Spitfire had lacked range and the Lockheed P-38 Lightning had proven inferior to the German planes at medium altitudes. That the daylight bombing program was possible at all was due largely to the Thunderbolts.

As the numbers of Thunderbolts and Mustangs serving in Europe increased, Thunderbolts were employed increasingly for low-level fighter-bomber missions. Armed with machine guns, bombs, and rockets, P-47's destroyed some 9,000 locomotives and 160,000 railroad cars and motorized vehicles. With the Hawker Typhoon, the P-47 was probably the greatest wartime fighter-bomber.

Thunderbolts destroyed a total of 11,874 enemy aircraft. The highest ranking American aces in Europe—Gabreski, Johnson, Zemke, Gentile and the rest—were Thunderbolt pilots. The famous 56th Fighter Group, the only 8th Air Force Fighter Group to persist in flying P-47's after the introduction of the Mustang, ended the war as America's second highest scoring fighter unit (1,006 kills) and enjoyed the most favorable ratio of losses to enemy aircraft destroyed in the ETO. In all theatres, Thunderbolts destroyed a total of 11,874 German and Japanese aircraft.

TECHNICAL NOTES: The Republic P-47B had a 2,000 h.p. P.&W. R-2800-21 air-cooled engine, a top speed of 429 m.p.h. at 30,000 ft., a span of 40.7 ft. and an armament of eight .50 cal. machine guns. The P-47L had a top speed of about 450 m.p.h.

The Hawker Typhoon

THE STORY OF THE HAWKER TYPHOON AND THE HAWKER TEMPEST IS one of two variations on a single design. In the end, the Typhoon owed its introduction into combat to the British need for countering the superiority of the German Focke-Wulf Fw 190 over the Spitfire. The Typhoon was first conceived, however, as a potential replacement for the Hawker Hurricane as early as 1937, before that airplane had even become operational! A good example of the feverish pace of competition for design supremacy in military aviation.

The Typhoon suffered a long gestation period, from 1937 to 1940. Then, just as it was about to be put into production, it was shunted aside when the grave war situation demanded full-scale manufacture of its predecessor, the Hurricane. Seven months later work on the Typhoon was resumed. The plane finally appeared in the spring of 1941. By the following September, Typhoons were in hot and heavy action with the Germans. They achieved almost immediate success over the Focke-Wulfs, particularly during the Dieppe operation and in combat over London in the course of Fw 190-escorted daylight bombing raids.

The Typhoon's major role, however, was to be offensive rather than defensive; and it was to make its highest marks as an air weapon employed against ground forces. After it proved its mettle in aerial combat, experiment by pilots revealed the Typhoon's ability to deal effectively with tanks and other land weapons. Thereafter, fitted with rocket launchers and equipped to carry bombs, Typhoons played havoc with German

Three Hawker Tempest Mk. V, series 2, fighters set out on a ground-attack mission. Under the wings of the Tempest in the foreground are launching racks for eight 60-lb. rockets.

The Hawker Typhoon Mk. IA (above) was designed to carry twelve .30 cal. machine guns in its wings. The more widely used Mk. IB mounted four 20mm. cannon.

The Westland Whirlwind was a precursor of the Typhoon. It did not, however, prove to be a successful fighter and only 112 were produced.

ground installations and armor in Normandy. The destruction of some 137 tanks credited to Typhoons at Avranches helped open the way for the liberation of France and Belgium.

In the meantime, work to improve the plane went on in the Hawker shops. A number of major modifications were made. These produced a radically changed Typhoon with greater range and speed. First designated Typhoon II, this improved version was latter named the Tempest. It went into service early in 1944, and met the test of combat two days after Operation Overlord got underway in France.

Upon introduction, the Tempest was the fastest low-medium altitude fighter on RAF duty. As such it became the anchor of British fighter defense against Germany's ingenious flying bomb—the V-1—which was first launched against England a week after D-day. Tempests accounted for 638 of the howling pilotless missiles in the first two months of their use.

TECHNICAL NOTES: The Hawker Typhoon had a 2,180 h.p. Sabre IIA liquid-cooled engine, a top speed of 405 m.p.h. at 18,000 ft., a span of 41.6 ft., an armament of four 20mm. cannon and two 1,000 lb. bombs or eight 60 lb. rocket projectiles. The Tempest V had a 2,200 h.p. Sabre IIB engine, a top speed of 435 m.p.h. at 17,000 ft., armament same as Typhoon.

The North American P-51 Mustang

THE NORTH AMERICAN P-51 MUSTANG HAS BEEN CALLED A LOT OF things, all good and well deserved. Without question, it was the finest American fighter to see service during World War II.

Ironically, the Mustang was conceived and produced at the request of the British. Early in 1940, the RAF asked the United States to come up with a substitute for the export version of Curtiss P-40 which had proven inadequate to combat conditions in Europe.

Of inspired design, the Mustang was built, tested, and placed in production in record time. Under the pressure of need, a prototype was built in 117 days and tested within seven months of the British request.

British-operated Mustangs saw first action in July, 1942, nobly acquitting themselves supporting assault troops at Dieppe the next month, and earning the distinction of being the first England-based single-engined fighter to thrust beyond the German border.

Until the Mustang came on the scene, American confidence had been placed in the P-47 Thunderbolt and P-38 Lightning. It was not until late 1943 that Mustangs marked with the star and bar went into action. The airplane was a winner from the first. High altitude escort and combat was its forte. And it had extreme range. Also, Mustang speed and maneuverability was superior to every piston-engine plane the Germans flew against it. Drawing upon the Mustang's talents beginning in March, 1944, the Eighth Air Force severely shook German morale by using Mustangs to escort mass formations of B-17 Fortresses and B-24 Lib-

The P-51D was the most widely produced of all Mustangs. This P-51D-30 has rocket launching stubs mounted under its wings.

Mustangs first saw combat with the RAF. This Mustang Mk. IA carried four .50 cal. machine guns in its wings and had a top speed of 390 m.p.h.

America's best operational fighter at the beginning of the war, the Curtiss P-40 was never a first-line aircraft. Shark-nosed P-40B's won fame, however, with the "Flying Tigers" in China, and did well as Tomahawk Mk. I's with the RAF in North Africa.

erators to Berlin and back. The days when *Luftwaffe* interceptors could attack daylight bombers beyond the range of the Allied escort fighters were over.

Like the Thunderbolt, the P-51 could be a formidable fighter-bomber. Flying at roof-top level or below (one P-51 returned to its English base with a turnip in its airscoop), the plane could deal rapid, stunning blows to enemy armor and troop concentrations and get away faster than the AA guns could track.

By the end of the War all but one of the 8th Air Force Fighter Groups (the 56th) had converted to P-51's, and the graceful Mustang is credited with having destroyed more enemy aircraft than any American fighter in the European Theatre of Operations. After converting to Mustangs, the famous 4th Fighter Group became the top-scorer in the ETO ending the war with a total of 1,016 enemy planes destroyed.

In the Pacific, 7th Air Force Mustangs based on Iwo Jima were the first Army fighters to operate over the Japanese home islands, while the 5th Air Force Mustangs scourged the skies over the Philippines in combat which nearly equaled the savagery of the air fighting in Europe.

A latecomer to European skies, the Mustang nevertheless accounted for more enemy aircraft than any other American fighter in the ETO. In two months in the spring of 1944, a single Mustang Group shot down 235 enemy planes and destroyed more than half as many more on the ground.

TECHNICAL NOTES: The North American P-51D had a 1,450 h.p. Merlin V-1650-7 liquid-cooled engine, a top speed of 437 m.p.h. at 25,000 ft., a span of 37 ft. and a standard armament of six .50 cal machine guns, plus up to two 1,000-lb. bombs or ten 5-inch HVAR rockets. Service ceiling was 40,000 ft.

The Mitsubishi A6M Zero-Sen

THE MAINSTAY OF JAPANESE AIR POWER FROM FIRST TO LAST DURING World War II, the famed Mitsubishi A6M Zero fighter was the first shipboard warplane capable of besting land-based opponents. As such, it keynoted a new era in naval aviation.

In 1941, from the flattops of the task force which Admiral Nagumo led to Pearl Harbor, Zeros flashed into prominence as the world's foremost carrier-based fighters. In the days that followed, throughout the Pacific, the appearance of Zeros over every major battle area fostered a legend of Japanese invincibility in the air.

Judged by contemporary Allied standards, the Zero was a warplane of exceptionally high calibre. It could maneuvre with the best, and had an excellent range: up to 1,130 miles—nearly twice that of the Spitfire which it equalled in size. In close combat, the Zero performed superbly. It appeared to flit like a hummingbird, but it stung like a wasp.

The Zero was first ordered by the Japanese Navy in 1937, and accepted for service two years later. It saw combat over China in August, 1940, where the late General Claire Chennault saw and appraised its abilities. He advised the USAAF to take notice, but his warning went unheeded. As a result, and because no example of the plane became available for study until mid-1942, the Zero was a deadly riddle to its enemies during the initial phase of the war.

No Allied fighter during the first year of the Pacific war could touch the Zero in the air. In Japan the *Zero-sen* became something of a national symbol of the triumph of Japanese arms.

Japan's greatest fighter was the A6M **Zero-sen.** The A6M5 Type O Mod. 52 was built for the Japanese Navy in larger numbers than any other variant. The example shown in this picture was captured by U. S. forces in the Pacific.

The Kawanishi NIKI-J **Shiden** Navy fighter (called "George" by U. S. flyers) was an excellent plane which appeared late in the war. It had four 20mm. cannon and two light machine guns and a top speed of 362 m.p.h.

The Kawasaki Ki. 61 **Hien** ("Tony") was one of the Japanese Army's standard fighters. It mounted two 20mm. cannon and two heavy machine guns and, in its most advanced variant, had a top speed of 373 m.p.h.

One of the many variants of the **Zero-sen** was the A6M2-N float-plane fighter.

But this was not to last. Successive modifications of the basic A6M design failed to develop rapidly enough. By 1943, the new American fighters had gained ascendancy, and the Japanese turned to other, more modern fighter types. Some of these, such as the Imperial Navy's Kawanishi N1K ("George") and the Army's Nakajima Ki. 84 ("Frank") were brilliant performers, the equal of America's best; but they appeared too late to have any substantial effect on the course of the Pacific air war.

A total of 10,938 Zeros were delivered to the Japanese Navy. In its early days, the Zero had been a vehicle for aces. Hiroyoshi Nishizawa, Japan's best, scored most of his 103 confirmed victories flying A6M's. And even in the last year of the war, its supremacy as a fighter forever lost, the Zero continued to be a formidable weapon. For, more than any other aircraft, it was the Zero which was used in the devastating *Kamikaze* attacks.

TECHNICAL NOTES: The Mitsubishi A6M5b had a 1,140 h.p. Nakajima Sakae 21 radial engine, a top speed of 351 m.p.h. at 19,000 ft., a span of 36 ft., a service ceiling of 33,000 ft. and an armament of one 7.7mm. and one 12.7mm. machine gun in the fuselage and four 20mm. cannon in the wings.

The Grumman F6F Hellcat

NOT THE LEAST OF AMERICA'S WORRIES IN THE GRIM MONTHS WHICH
followed Pearl Harbor was the fact that no U.S. fighter was capable of
dealing with the Japanese Zero. The USAAF fighters, even if they had
been a match for the Zero—and they were not—had no Western Pacific
bases from which to operate. The Navy's carrier forces were still largely
intact, but they were heavily outnumbered by their Japanese counterparts, and the standard U.S. Navy fighter, the barrel-shaped Grumman
Wildcat, was painfully inferior to the brilliant Mitsubishi.

The Navy's hopes were focused on two designs, the Grumman F6F
Hellcat and the Vought F4U Corsair. The Corsair had first been flown
in 1940 and had proven to be an aircraft of exceptional promise, but
early versions had been full of "bugs" and pre-production delays set in.
Navy officials, apprehensive that the Corsair might prove unsuitable for
carrier-based operations, turned to the Grumman Aircraft Company.

Since Pearl Harbor, Grumman had been working feverishly on a
replacement for the Wildcat. The resulting design, the F6F Hellcat, was
flown in August, 1942, and almost immediately placed in production.
Within a year Hellcats were operating from the decks of the new *Essex*-
class carriers and in September, 1943, they went into action over the
Gilberts.

The Hellcat had been created specifically to master the Zero, and
in this it proved eminently successful: it was faster, more maneuverable,
more rugged, higher flying, and better armed. The Navy, without delay,
designated it the standard U.S. carrier fighter.

The most widely produced U. S. Navy fighter was the Grumman
F6F-3 Hellcat. In this picture, Hellcats aboard U.S.S. **Bunker Hill**
have just received the order "Pilots man your planes."

The best U. S. Navy fighter was the Chance Vought F4U Corsair. It was the first operational U. S. fighter to have a maximum speed greater than 400 m.p.h.

The standard U. S. Navy fighter at the beginning of World War II was the Grumman F4F-4 Wildcat. With a top speed of only 284 m.p.h., it was no match for the **Zero-sen.**

It was the Hellcat, then, which bore the major share of responsibility for destroying the Japanese air forces. In the wild air battle over the Marianas in June, 1944, Hellcats shot down over 400 enemy aircraft and eliminated most of the elite cadres of Japanese naval fighter pilots. By 1945, the ratio of Japanese to American losses had risen to 21.6 to 1. The Navy's leading Hellcat ace, Commander David McCampbell of *Essex*'s famous Air Group 15, shot down 34 Japanese planes and destroyed 21 more on the ground during a single tour of duty. Of the 9,282 Japanese aircraft shot down during the war, the majority were accounted for by Hellcats.

Meanwhile, the Corsair, which had been diverted to shore-based duty with the Marines, had developed into a superb aircraft, superior even to the Hellcat. Corsairs went into action from bases in Guadalcanal in 1943 and rapidly earned a reputation among the Japanese as the most formidable of all U.S. fighters. Even though they did not begin to operate from carrier flight decks until late in the war, Corsairs were responsible for shooting down some 2,140 Japanese planes before VJ Day.

Indeed, the F4U was such an exceptional design that it was one of the few wartime airplanes maintained in production after the war. Corsairs fought in Korea, in an air war where fighter operations were almost entirely conducted by 700-mile-an-hour jets. In August, 1952, a Corsair even contrived to down a Russian MIG-15, and there is a sort of nostalgic justice in the curious fact that the only Navy ace in the Korean conflict made all his kills flying an F4U-5N Corsair.

TECHNICAL NOTES: The Grumman F6F-3 had a 2,000 h.p. P.&W. R-2800-10W air-cooled engine, a top speed of 371 m.p.h., a span of 42.8 ft. and an armament of six .50 cal. machine guns. The Vought F4U-1 had a 2,000 h.p. P.&W. R-2800-8 air-cooled engine, a top speed of 417 m.p.h., a span of 41 ft. and armament of six .50 cal. machine guns. The F4U-4 had a top speed of 450 m.p.h.

The Messerschmitt Me 262 Schwalbe

IN AVIATION HISTORY, THE REDOUBTABLE MESSERSCHMITT ME 262 ranks as an unquestionable "first." It was the first military jet-propelled combat airplane, and the only plane of its type to see important action in World War II.

Development of the Me 262 was initiated in the fall of 1938. It proceeded slowly, hampered by high-level opposition from both the German Air Ministry and the *Luftwaffe*. But Messerschmitt and his design team persisted. An experimental model was flown in April, 1941, and a spark of Air Ministry enthusiasm resulted in a green light to continue development on a larger scale. Official apathy did not, however, fade completely, for the best Messerschmitt was allowed was a twenty-plane order. The simple fact was that no real need for the unique plane was foreseen.

Berlin's tune changed when a Me 262 was demonstrated for Goering, who convinced Hitler that the plane should be used. The extent of Allied bombing had filled the German dictator with the desire to retaliate. Hitler wanted bombers, and though told that the Me 262 was a fighter, he proclaimed it a bomber and ordered it to be produced as such.

Hitler's decision, apart from delaying tactical employment of the Me 262 for at least four months, was technically absurd. The plane was never designed to operate at low altitudes and had a comparatively short duration of flight. Moreover, the modifications required to convert the *Schwalbe* into an attack bomber so reduced its speed as to bring it within range of the newer Allied piston-engine fighters.

The Messerschmitt Me 262 **Schwalbe** was the world's first operational jet fighter. This Me 262A-1a was surrendered by its pilot to American forces in Frankfurt.

The Messerschmitt Me 163B **Komet** was the world's first rocket-powered fighter. Some versions of the **Komet** carried rocket missiles which fired vertically upwards from the wings.

The Arado Ar 234 **Blitz** was an extraordinarily good twin-jet bomber which was developed too late to make any important contribution to the **Luftwaffe.**

General of Fighters Adolph Galland bitterly protested the modification and was removed from his Command for his trouble. But the logic of the situation, coupled with the enormity of the Allied daylight bombing offensive, at last prevailed over Hitler's objections, and the Me 262 was hastily redeployed for its originally-intended role as an interceptor.

By World War II standards, the aircraft's performance bordered on the incredible. With the assistance of a rocket booster it could climb to an altitude of 38,400 ft, from a standing start in 4.5 minutes. It had a maximum speed of 540 m.p.h. at that altitude. And even by jet aviation standards, the design and construction of the Me 262 manifested a sophistication not fully attained by the Allies until several years after VE Day.

In the desperate months before the collapse of Germany, the *Luftwaffe* frantically tested a number of other jet and rocket-propelled aircraft. Some were merely bizarre and some, like the Arado 234 jet bomber, were amazingly advanced. But only one saw even minimally significant service. This was the Messerschmitt Me 163 *Komet*. The *Komet* was a weird little 600 m.p.h. rocket-driven fighter; the world's first. It had a flight duration of only eight minutes and more of its pilots were killed by take-off and landing accidents than by Allied gunfire; but it was sufficiently formidable to warrant some intensive—and effective—air raids on its places of manufacture.

The *Schwalbe* and the *Komet* were brilliant eleventh-hour products of German scientific genius. Neither significantly affected the course of the war, but both had a profound influence on the subsequent development of military aviation.

TECHNICAL NOTES: The Messerschmitt Me 262A-1A was powered by two 1,980 lbs. s.t. Jumo 004B-1 turbojet engines, had a top speed of 540 m.p.h. at 19,684 ft., a span of 41 ft. and an armament of four 30mm. cannon and twenty-four 50mm. rocket missiles.

The Junkers Ju 87 Stuka

IN A WARTIME JINGLE WRITTEN FOR AIRCRAFT SPOTTERS, THE BRITISH cartoonist Wren described the German *Stuka* thus:

> A crooked wing, a square-cut tail,
> Fat legs below and a bomb to trail,
> Deep-jowled before a glasshouse hump,
> The Stuka's an unshapely lump.

The British could afford to be a little complacent about the Junkers Ju 87 in 1941. The Battle of Britain had demonstrated the German dive bomber's terrible vulnerability to British fighters. But in the opening phases of the war, the *Stuka* had made itself one of the most feared weapons in the German arsenal.

In the early 1930's, *Luftwaffe* opinion had been divided on the subject of dive bombing. Various dive bomber prototypes were tested under the most rigorous conditions and it was with some reluctance that the Ju 87 was finally ordered into production in 1936. In 1938, the *Luftwaffe* had an opportunity to "field-test" the machine in Spain. Here its combat record proved so astonishingly good that production was sharply stepped up.

When Germany attacked Poland in 1939, *Stukas* were largely responsible for the obliteration of Polish air and tank forces on the ground. Later, operating in close cooperation with the panzer units, *Stukas* smashed Belgian forts in a matter of hours, shattered French and Dutch

The Junkers Ju 87 **Stuka** dive bomber was one of the most feared German planes in the early part of the war. Its extreme vulnerability to enemy fighters was exposed, however, in the Battle of Britain.

The twin-engine Junkers Ju 88 was one of the best all-round aircraft of the war. It served as a dive, level and torpedo bomber,
a fighter and a reconnaissance plane. The Ju 88A-4 shown above
had a 273 m.p.h. top speed. One late-war variant, the JU 188S-1,
hit 429 m.p.h.

Like circling vultures, a cluster of **Stuka**'s begin to peel off for an
attack on French infantry.

supply and communication lines and harried British troops on the beaches
at Dunkirk.

Shrewdly abetted by German propaganda, the *Stuka*'s reputation
swelled to unwarranted proportions. It was called invincible, a weapon
that defeated whole nations. And even without advance publicity, there
is no doubt that the *Stuka's* psychological effect on troops under attack
was unnerving. The ugly plane's configuration had a disturbingly vul-
turish aspect, and when diving, the *Stuka*'s engine emitted a harrowing
whine. Above all, the *Stuka* was, in fact, a very accurate bomber.

But when the *Stukas* encountered RAF fighter opposition over
England, their low speed and light armament made the Ju 87's into
suicide planes. In the summer of 1940, the *Luftwaffe* was forced to with-
draw *Stukas* from the air battle over Britain.

Ju 87's were, however, used effectively on other fronts—in the Balkans, Crete, North Africa, Russia, and along the Mediterranean and
North Sea convoy routes. But the *Stuka* never recovered its reputation.
As the war progressed the *Stuka*'s duties were increasingly assumed by
other aircraft—especially by the *Luftwaffe*'s fine, versatile medium
bomber, the Junkers Ju 88.

TECHNICAL NOTES: The Junkers Ju 87B
had a 1,100 h.p. Jumo 211 Da
liquid-cooled engine, a top speed
of 232 m.p.h., a span of 45.2 ft.
and an armament of three 7.9mm.
machine guns and up to 1,100 lbs.
of bombs. The twin-engine
Ju 88A-4 had a top speed of 273
m.p.h. and an armament of five
7.9mm. machine guns and up to
3,300 lbs. of bombs.

The Douglas SBD Dauntless

IN SO FAR AS ANY TECHNIQUE OF AIR COMBAT CAN BE ASCRIBED, DIVE bombing was the invention of the U.S. Navy. Experiments with the technique were conducted as early as 1919, and by the 1930's, dive bombing had become a staple of U.S. Naval Air Operations. From the tactical doctrines hammered out in Curtiss Helldivers and BT-1's came many of the methods which were subsequently to be used by the air-forces of all the great powers.

The Navy's emphasis on dive bombing stemmed from a conviction that level bombing from medium and high altitudes would prove ineffective against rapidly maneuvering targets such as ships. The correctness of this assumption was to be demonstrated many times over during the war.

The standard Navy dive bomber from the beginning to the end of World War II was the hardy Douglas SBD Dauntless. None of the usual technical statistics about the plane suggest its greatness, but then dive-bomber specifications seldom do. The Dauntless was slow, lightly armed and lacking in range, but it was a comparatively swift and superbly stable diver. And that, experience showed, was the main thing.

The SBD can only be evaluated in terms of what it did. Until 1944 SBD's led all other arms of the service in tonnage of enemy warships sunk. In one 29-month period alone, SBD's flew 1,189,476 operational hours. Yet the Dauntless enjoyed the lowest ratio of loss of any Navy plane.

The U. S. Navy's Douglas SBD was probably the greatest dive bomber of the war. It proved to be the crucial weapon at the decisive Battle of Midway.

Japan's principal dive bomber during the first half of the war was the Navy's Aichi D3A1 ("Val") which participated in the attack on Pearl Harbor.

Late in the war SBD's were supplemented by Curtiss SB2C Helldivers. They were not markedly superior to the SBD's.

If the Dauntless had done nothing but participate in the Battle of Midway, however, its fame would be secure. For it was there that the SBD's from the carriers *Enterprise, Hornet* and *Yorktown* turned the tide of the war.

The great Japanese armada which advanced on Midway in June, 1942, was bent on finishing the work begun at Pearl Harbor: the destruction of the U.S. Pacific Fleet. With their massive force of four heavy carriers, eleven battleships and ten cruisers, the Japanese vastly outnumbered the American units hastily assembled under Admirals Fletcher and Spruance. And the opening phases of the battle—unsuccessful attacks by U.S. shore-based aircraft and carrier-based torpedo bombers—seemed merely to confirm the inevitable.

Then the SBD's appeared over the Japanese force. In five minutes they sank three carriers (one of which was also hit by torpedoes fired by the U.S. submarine *Nautilus*) and a few hours later sank the fourth. For good measure, they also sank one heavy cruiser and so badly damaged another that it was out of commission for two years. The remainder of the Japanese battle fleet retired to the west.

Neither the Americans nor the Japanese immediately grasped the full significance of Midway. In retrospect, however, its meaning is clear. Its calamitously deprived Japan of the one thing which might possibly have saved her from ultimate ruin: a decisive victory before the full industrial might of the United States could be thrown on the scales.

TECHNICAL NOTES: The Douglas SBD-3 had a 950 h.p. Wright R-1820-52 air-cooled engine, a top speed of 255 m.p.h., a span of 41 ft. and an armament of two .30 cal. and two .50 cal. machine guns and up to 1,000 lbs. of bombs.

The Fairey Swordfish

THE BRITISH CARRIER-BASED FAIREY SWORDFISH TORPEDO BOMBER WAS the paradox of Royal Navy air power throughout the first half of the war in Europe. In contrast to its contemporaries, the Spitfire and Hurricane, the Swordfish was practically obsolete when it was accepted for service in 1936. By the time hostilities commenced the plane was outmoded by nearly everything flying. It was a fabric-covered biplane with open cockpits, and carried a crew of two whose defense consisted of one fixed forward-firing Vickers light machine gun and one maneuverable Lewis light machine gun. An 18-inch torpedo was slung between the struts of a fixed undercarriage. At an altitude of 7,000 feet, the Swordfish's top speed was 138 m.p.h. and landed at 67 m.p.h. The airplane was a direct, little-modified descendant of the Spad, SE-5 Scout, and all other kite-like planes of World War I.

However, the antique appearance of the plane was deceptive. Performance, not looks, is what counts in battle. The "String Bag," as its pilots affectionately called the Swordfish, performed brilliantly. The abilities which rendered it obsolete by normal standards made the plane a phenomenal success in its job. The tremendous lift of its double span of wings and the steady, relentless pull of its slow airscrew could put the Swordfish into the air from a flight deck under the worst of weather conditions. Its slow-flying enabled it to launch a torpedo with peerless accuracy.

When the mammoth German battleship *Bismarck* was at bay off

The Royal Navy's Fairey Swordfish was an anomaly. The least modern of torpedo bombers, it was the most successful. It inflicted great damage on both the Italian and German navies.

America's foremost torpedo bomber was designed by Grumman and was originally known as the TBF. The majority produced were built by General Motors, however, and were designated as TBM's.

Japan's most famous torpedo bomber was the Nakajima B5N1 ("Kate"). Along with **Zero-sen** fighters and Aichi dive bombers, B5N's participated in the Pearl Harbor attack.

Brest, hemmed in by a closing ring of British battleships, cruisers, destroyers and carriers, Swordfish from the latter spearheaded her defeat and death. They got aloft and into action even when the bow of one carrier was rising and falling as much as sixty feet in heavy seas. It was a Swordfish torpedo which struck and disabled *Bismarck*'s rudder and caused her to circle like a target in a shooting gallery while the guns of her enemies pounded her to death.

The greatest victory achieved by Swordfish was, however, in the Mediterranean. On the night of November 11, 1940, Swordfish from the carrier *Illustrious* struck a devastating blow at the Italian heavy naval units anchored in Taranto harbor. Score: one battleship sunk and two others wrecked.

Swordfish participated in many other gallant actions, both in the Mediterranean and the Atlantic. And if none was as impressive as Taranto, at least one was completely characteristic of the fabulous history of the queer old plane. At Bomba Bay, near Tobruk, Swordfish from the carrier *Eagle* attacked a group of enemy transports. Three torpedoes struck home. Four ships went down. For the Swordfish, the incredible was merely typical.

TECHNICAL NOTES: The Fairey Swordfish II had a 750 h.p. Pegasus 30 air-cooled engine, a top speed of 138 m.p.h., a span of 45.5 ft. and an armament of two .30 cal. machine guns and one 18-inch torpedo. The Grumman TBM had a top speed of 278 m.p.h., three .50 cal. and one .30 cal. machine guns and one 21-inch torpedo.

The Illyushin IL-2 Stormovik

THE SOVIET AIR FORCE IN WORLD WAR II WAS CONSIDERABLY BETTER than most people in the West yet realize. Certainly it was—or came to be —far better than the Germans had any reason to expect when they invaded Russia in the spring of 1941. Everything at that time suggested that Russian military aviation was second rate. The *Mosca* and *Chato* fighters and ZKB bombers which the Soviets sent to Spain in the 1930's were obviously inferior to the Messerschmitts and Dorniers. The performance of the Soviet Air Force against the motley Finnish fighter squadrons during the Winter War was lamentable. And the effect of Soviet aviation in resisting the Germans' sweep across Russia in 1941 was negligeable.

But by 1942, while German ground forces struggled through stiffening resistance towards the debacle at Stalingrad, new Soviet equipment had begun to appear in the air over Russia. The Russian plane which first caught the world's imagination was an odd-looking attack bomber called the *Stormovik*.

Designed by Sergei Illyushin, who won a 200,000-rouble Stalin prize for his efforts, the IL-2 *Stormovik* exemplified the Russian tactical doctrine which called for employment of aircraft primarily in close cooperation with ground forces. The Russians thus stressed attack, dive bombings, and low-altitude fighter operations. Strategic bombing and high-altitude work of all sorts were neglected.

The *Stormovik* was a tank-destroyer. It was armed with two 20mm.

A flight of Illyushin IL-10 **Stormovik**'s, on their way to attack German ground forces, skim low over the hills of Southern Russia. The IL-10 was an improved version of the original IL-2. It had a 335 m.p.h. top speed, mounted two 23mm. cannon and two 7.62mm. machine guns and carried a 2,000-lb. bomb load.

Crude in some details such as radio and gunsights, the YAK-3 was nevertheless a very good fighter. Designed to operate most effectively at low altitudes, it had a top speed of 403 m.p.h.

The Petlyakov PE-2 was an excellent 340 m.p.h. light bomber. It was the Russian equivalent of the American A-20 and the British Mosquito.

Yakovlev YAK-9D fighters such as these were used to escort USAAF bombers to and from Russian bases on shuttle raids. Improved YAK-9's continued in service until the Korean War.

cannon and two 7.62mm. machine guns mounted in the wings and carried a heavy load of 880 lb. bombs or aerial rockets. Massive armor plate protected the plane's engine and cockpit against the ground fire which could be expected while the *Stormovik* operated at low levels. Working in unescorted pairs, the *Stormoviks* inflicted considerable damage on German panzer units during the middle war years.

Concurrently with the *Stormovik's* debut, the new generation of Soviet fighters began to appear in action. At first these aircraft were still well below German standards, but Russian designers rapidly improved their fighting qualities. By 1943, with the introduction of the radial-engined LA-7 and the in-line-engined YAK-9, Soviet fighter forces began to approach qualitative parity with the *Luftwaffe*. Ivan Kojedub, with 62 victories Russia's top ace, flew an LA-7.

By the end of the war, the Soviet Air Force had become both large and qualitatively good. Free French pilots of the Normandie-Nieman Groupe de Chasse flying in Russia called the Soviet YAK-3 fighter superior to both the Messerschmitt Bf 109G and Focke-Wulf 109A at low and medium altitudes. The twin-engined PE-2 was an attack bomber comparable to the American Douglas A-20A or the German Junkers Ju 88. And even before VE Day, Russian designers were busily experimenting with rocket- and ram jet- propelled fighter planes.

TECHNICAL NOTES: The Illyushin IL-2 had a 1,600 h.p. AM-38F liquid-cooled engine, a top speed of 257 m.p.h., a span of 47.8 ft. and an armament of two 7.62mm. and one 12.7mm. machine guns and two 20mm. cannon and up to 800 lbs. of bombs. The IL-10 had a top speed of 355 m.p.h. and could carry up to 2,000 lbs. of bombs.

The de Havilland Mosquito

BRITAIN'S SLEEK, FAST TWIN-ENGINED DE HAVILLAND MOSQUITO WON fame both as a fighter and as a bomber. It was originally designed wholly at the initiative of the de Havilland Company, and for a time it appeared that the RAF might not accept the plane for service. But the Mosquito's performance during test flights was so phenomenal that official reluctance was soon overcome.

For the Allies, the Mosquito attack bomber achieved all the results that Germany had hoped to realize with the Junkers Ju 87. The British plane was a masterpiece in concept and design created to fulfill what was then a revolutionary offensive premise: that a bomber could be effective when its only defense was an ability to outrun intercepting fighters. Once put to the test, the Mosquito proved the premise valid.

Constructed entirely of wood, the airplane was astonishingly agile. It performed with a superb combination of abilities not often achieved all in one airplane. The Mosquito was maneuverable to that high degree where pilot and plane seem to be one. It could fly faster than most fighters dispatched against it, and it could dive-bomb with amazing accuracy. Its combat record fully sustains the claim that the plane was one of the most potent weapons at the command of the RAF during World War II.

The exploits of the Mosquito were almost legendary. Both as a bomber and a fighter, the plane took a leading role in almost every type of combat pertinent to a warplane. Mosquito attack bombers declared open season on Berlin and hammered the German capital day and night

This sleek de Havilland Mosquito Mk. XVI of No. 571 Squadron served as a pathfinder for the RAF's big nighttime bombers. Fighter versions of the Mosquito had "solid" noses which housed four 20mm. cannon and four .303 cal. machine guns.

The Douglas A-20 was the standard American twin-engine attack bomber. A fighter variant, the A-20G, had a dorsal turret and two .50 cal. machine guns and four 20mm. cannon in the nose. The Douglas was slower than the Mosquito and carried a smaller bomb load.

Black and white identification stripes were painted on Allied aircraft participating in Operation Overlord. The Martin B-26G shown below was used both as an attack bomber and as a medium altitude bomber.

in a series of 320 raids in 1944–45. As many as one hundred per raid took part, each carrying half a ton more bombload than a B-17—and flying 50 m.p.h. faster! Flying only a few feet above the water, Mosquitos laid an effective mine-screen in the Kiel Canal. They lobbed 4,000-lb. bombs into the mouths of German railroad tunnels and slapped V-1 launching sites to oblivion.

One sensational feat that put the Mosquito on the front pages was the destruction of Gestapo headquarters in Oslo. Zooming in at roof-top height, Mosquitos put their bombs into the building through its windows and roared away to safety as the target exploded and collapsed like a house of cards.

As a fighter, the Mosquito's activities and results were just as spectacular. They accounted for more than 1,200 enemy aircraft and V-1's over England. One actually fought and won an artillery duel with an enemy destroyer, rendering it defenseless by firing a barrage of armor-piercing shells into its furnaces and turbines from beyond the range of the ship's anti-aircraft.

TECHNICAL NOTES: The de Havilland Mosquito Mk. XVI had two 1,710 h.p. Merlin 73 liquid-cooled engines, a top speed of 408 m.p.h. at 26,000 ft., a span of 54.2 ft., and carried up to 4,000 lbs. of bombs. The Douglas A-20G had a top speed of 317 m.p.h. and carried up to 4,000 lbs. of bombs.

The Mitsubishi G4M

THE UBIQUITOUS MITSUBISHI G4M WAS PROBABLY THE MOST VERSATILE of Japan's war-time medium bombers. It was used for level bombing, torpedo bombing, photo reconnaissance and night fighting. Designed as a land based aircraft, it could, like the American B-25, be adapted for launching from the flight decks of large carriers. G4M's were produced in large quantities and served, from the beginning to the end of the war, in every part of the Pacific.

Code named "Betty" by the Allies, G4M's first appeared in action over China in May, 1941. They were in the thick of things almost immediately after Pearl Harbor. They were largely responsible for smashing American air strength on the ground at Clark Field in the Philippines, and on December 8, 1941, they shared honors with G3M torpedo bombers in sinking H.M.S. *Repulse* and *Prince of Wales*—Britain's two principal capital ships in Asian waters. Subsequently G4M's appeared in combat nearly everywhere: New Guinea, New Britain, New Georgia, the Solomons, the Kuriles, the Marshalls, the Marianas, the Gilberts and so on and on.

Early versions of the G4M were somewhat slow and clumsy, but modification soon brought the plane's performance up to levels attained by the leading Allied medium bombers. The Japanese were particularly pleased with the G4M2's 2,262-mile range and its military load of up to 2,200 pounds of bombs or torpedoes.

But the G4M had one serious weakness. Its self-sealing fuel tanks

A flight of Japanese Navy Mitsubishi G4M1 Type 1 Mod. 11 ("Betty") bombers, the type which sank H.M.S. **Repulse** and **Prince of Wales** on December 8, 1941. Later versions of the aircraft mounted a dorsal turret.

The Japanese Army's best bomber was the Mitsubishi Ki.67 **Hiryu** ("Peggy"). A late-war design, it was highly versatile. The Ki.67's in this picture are marked with green crosses painted on all Japanese warplanes after VJ-day.

Most Japanese Army medium bombers, such as this Mitsubishi Ki.21-IIb ("Sally") were slow and vulnerable to enemy fighters.

proved ineffective and the plane was highly inflammable. The Japanese pilots called the G4M the "Flying Cigar." The soubriquet did not refer solely to the plane's tapered, cylindrical shape. By 1944, the number of G4M's which had fallen in flames before American ground and air fire had reached alarming proportions.

Nevertheless, the Japanese Navy continued to use G4M's effectively until VJ Day. In the final days of the Pacific War, G4M's were adapted as "mother planes" for the dreadful *Oka*'s, the tiny jet propelled flying bombs which *Kamikaze* pilots used so devastatingly against the U. S. Navy.

TECHNICAL NOTES: The Mitsubishi G4M1 had two 1,530 h.p. Kasei air-cooled engines, a top speed of 266 m.p.h., a span of 81.6 ft. and an armament of four 7.7mm. machine guns and one 20mm. cannon and up to 2,200 lbs. of bombs. The Ki 67 had a top speed of 335 m.p.h. and carried up to 1,760 lbs. of bombs.

The North American B-25 Mitchell

THE NORTH AMERICAN B-25 LIGHT-MEDIUM BOMBER EARNED MANY laurels. Named after Colonel William "Billy" Mitchell, the airplane helped to vindicate his outspoken, prophetic views on air power. It served with distinction on every battle front during the war. Most of all, the B-25 was the plane which first revealed the vulnerability of the Japanese home islands to aerial attack.

Developed prior to the entry of the United States into the war, the B-25 went on active duty the middle of 1941. After Pearl Harbor, it was placed on anti-submarine patrol over the Pacific. On such duty, a B-25 became the first American twin-engined bomber to sink one of Japan's underwater shipkillers.

Because of its over-all range of twelve hundred miles—attainable while carrying over a ton and a half of bombs—and its ability to take off in so short a distance as the deck of a flattop, the B-25 was selected to implement the bold stroke of bombing Tokyo in April, 1942. Under the command of then Lt. Col. James H. Doolittle, sixteen Mitchells roared off the flight deck of U.S.S. *Hornet* to serve notice that the war could come to heart of Japan. This act alone earned the B-25 its niche in history. Striking at a time when Japan was flush, almost complacent, with the victories achieved in the four months following Pearl Harbor, the B-25's boosted American morale and helped set in train a revision of Japanese strategy which led to overextension and defeat for Japan. Less helpfully, the raid also served to bring about a strengthening of Japanese air defenses which was to be felt keenly by USAAF bombers later.

The North American B-25's in this picture illustrate three design variants. Nearest the camera is a B-25J bomber. Next is a B-25J fighter-bomber with eight .50 cal. machine guns in its nose. Farthest away is a B-25H attack bomber with four .50 cal. machine guns and a 75mm. cannon in its nose.

B-25B's such as this were used in the Doolittle raid on Tokyo.

Germany's standard medium bomber during the Battle of Britain was the Heinkel He 111P (shown here with RAF markings).

One of Germany's best medium bombers was the Dornier Do 217E which first began to appear in action in 1941.

As the war progressed, Mitchells came to be used for nearly every role appropriate to a bomber: high- and low-level bombing, strafing, photo reconnaissance, and submarine patrol. And the B-25H fighter-bomber was the most heavily armed airplane ever built: fourteen .50 cal. machine guns and a huge 75mm cannon.

The stalwart also did yeoman work in Europe. The RAF put it to good use in tactical bombing operations beginning in January, 1943. Russia, too, profited from the abilities of the plane. More than 800 were flight-delivered to the SAF.

The B-25 Mitchell was probably the best medium bomber of the war. Potent and versatile, it served long and well, and established a reputation for service that few planes of any type could match.

TECHNICAL NOTES: The B-25B had two 1,700 h.p. Wright R-2600-9 air-cooled engines, a top speed of 320 m.p.h., a span of 67.5 ft. and an armament of four .50 cal. and one .30 cal. machine guns and up to 3,600 lbs. of bombs.

The Boeing B-17 Flying Fortress

THE MAINSTAY OF THE HUGE ALLIED DAYLIGHT BOMBING OFFENSIVE against Germany was perhaps the most famous of all American warplanes: the B-17 Flying Fortress.

The first Fortress was completed in July, 1935 and impressed military observers by flying non-stop from Seattle, Washington to Dayton, Ohio—a distance of 2,100 miles—at an average speed of 252 m.p.h. But pre-war procurement being what it was, by the summer of 1939 only 13 B-17's had been delivered to the USAAF.

Export B-17C's first saw action with the RAF in 1941, but the plane proved to be slow, clumsy and under-gunned, and the British soon discontinued its use. It has been suggested that this early negative experience with the Fortress had some bearing on the British decision to abandon daylight bombing in favor of nighttime "saturation" raids.

The USAAF, however, was wholeheartedly committed to daylight precision bombing, and work on improved versions of the B-17 went ahead. By the end of 1941, the radically altered B-17E was in production and within a few months was in action in the Pacific. The B-17E differed from earlier Forts both in its enlarged and redesigned tail assembly and in its heavy increase in defensive armament. It had a tail-gunner's position mounting twin .50 cal. Brownings, power-operated ventral and dorsal turrets and individual flexible machine gun mounts in the radio and navigation compartments. The B-17 was, in truth, beginning to live up to its nickname. On the first all-American bombing raid

A Boeing B-17F of the 97th Bomber Group flies over the rugged mountains of North Africa. The effective combat radius of the B-17F was about 800 miles.

A B-17G, with distinctive "chin" turret, trundles off its airfield. As the war drew to an end the USAAF ceased painting its war planes in camouflage colors.

When this photograph was taken, this 8th Air Force B-24H Liberator had flown 77 missions. More Liberators than B-17's were produced, but the later versions of the B-17 were preferred for the dangerous raids over Germany.

The B-17B was slightly modified for use by the RAF. In combat, as the B-17C, it was not a success.

against the Germans in August, 1942, B-17E's successfully hit their target at Rouen, effectively dealt with enemy fighter opposition, and returned to England without casualties.

In the succeeding months the Fortresses often sustained heavy combat losses but the daylight bombing offensive steadily mounted in size and fury. With the advent of B-17F's and G's, the Fortress almost completely replaced the four-engine consolidated B-24, the USAAF's other standard heavy bomber, in the Eighth Air Force squadrons assigned to European targets. By the beginning of 1944, so many Fortresses were available that more than 1,000 could be allocated for individual raids.

Despite the combat losses suffered by the Fortresses, the planes were formidable air weapons. B-17's shot down almost twice as many enemy aircraft per 1,000 sorties as the highest scoring USAAF fighters. Between 1943 and 1945, they poured a total of 640,036 tons of explosives on European targets.

TECHNICAL NOTES: The Boeing B-17G had four 1,380 h.p. Wright GR-1820-97 air-cooled engines, a top speed of 300 m.p.h. at 30,000 ft., a span of 103.6 ft. and an armament of thirteen .50 cal. machine guns and up to 17,600 lbs. for short ranges or 4,000 lbs. for long ranges.

The Avro Lancaster

WHEREAS AMERICAN DOCTRINE CALLED FOR DAYLIGHT PRECISION bombing, Britain favored nighttime "saturation" of military and industrial target areas. The American method was more accurate and more dangerous; the British method was safer and more wasteful of bombs. Which was more effective is still hotly debated.

This distinction in technique accounts for some of the dissimilarities between the B-17 and its British counterpart, the four-engined Avro Lancaster. The Lancaster was more lightly armed, had a lower service ceiling and carried a vastly greater tonnage of bombs. Indeed, the Lancaster's bomb-carrying ability exceeded even that of the gigantic B-29 Superfortress. One Lancaster could lift and deliver the awesome 22,000-lb. "Grand Slam" deep penetration bomb perfected by the British shortly before the war ended.

But no specialty of mission could explain the Lancaster's remarkable flying characteristics. The plane almost handled like a fighter. It could dive-bomb, barrel-roll and perform a complete loop fully loaded (a maneuver not, however, to be advised).

The first heavy bomber to carry the war into the heart of Germany, the Lancaster went on active duty with the RAF in April, 1942. It began its long, effective career carrying 4,000-lb. bombs, was graduated to 8,000 pounders, then to carrying 12,000 pounders. According to the wartime commander of the RAF Bomber Command, Sir Arthur Harris, the efficiency of the Lancaster "was almost incredible, both in perform-

The Avro Lancaster was the greatest of Britain's heavy bombers. This Lancaster Mk. I was the standard version; special fuselage modifications were required for those Lancasters which carried the 12,000-lb. "Tallboy" bomb.

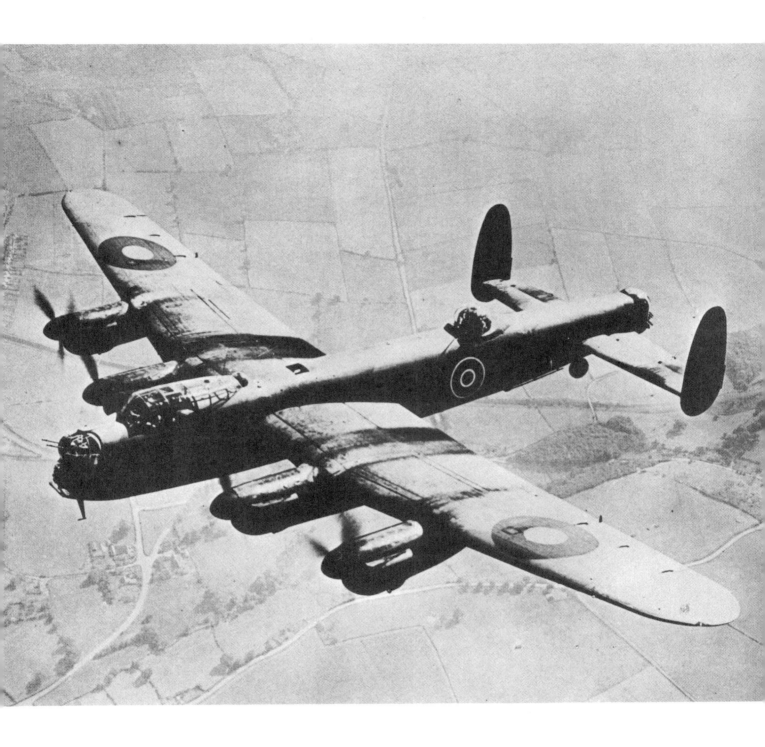

Mainstay of the RAF Bomber Command in the early days of the war was the sturdy old Vickers Wellington.

The first of the RAF's big four-engine nighttime bombers was the slab-sided Short Stirling. It could carry a maximum bomb load of 14,000 lb.

The Handley Page Halifax carried a slightly smaller bomb load than the Stirling and Lancaster but was suitable for a wider variety of roles.

ance and in the way it could be saddled with ever-increasing loads without breaking the 'camel's back.' " With understandable prejudice, he praised the able plane as "the finest bomber of the war!" Once on active duty, the Lancaster rapidly rose to become the RAF's major offensive weapon, delivering nearly two-thirds of the bombs dropped by the RAF on Germany. It was particularly effective in destroying the main sources of Germany's heavy industry hydro-electric power in the Ruhr. A high point of the Lancaster's combat career was reached in September, 1944, when a group of the bombers made a bold daylight attack on the formidable German battleship *Tirpitz* as she lay in Norway's Kaa Fjord. Britain had previously tried every means possible to knock out the massive 45,000-ton pride of the German Navy, including midget submarines and frogmen, but to no avail. Lancasters, carrying 12,000-lb. deep-penetration bombs called "Tallboys," finally sank the battleship. They hit her first on September 15, but poor visibility robbed them of success. Intelligence reported that only one bomb found its mark and that the ship was on the move to Tromso Fjord. Just less than a month later, thirty-one Lancasters caught up with her there, came in at 14,000 feet, let loose their "Tallboys" and sank her. The destruction of the ship virtually ended the threat of the German surface fleet.

TECHNICAL NOTES: The Avro Lancaster Mk. I had four 1,640 h.p. Merlin XX liquid-cooled engines, a top speed of 287 m.p.h. at 11,500 ft., a span of 102 ft. and an armament of eight .303 cal. machine guns and up to 14,000 lbs. of bombs. The modified Lancaster III could carry the 22,000 lb. "Grand Slam" bomb.

The Boeing B-29 Superfortress

THE FAME OF THE BOEING B-29 SUPERFORTRESS AS A FORMIDABLE AIR weapon began in June, 1944, when the gigantic heavy bomber was first employed against the Japanese homeland. It quickly became one of the principal weapons used by the Allies in the Pacific Theatre.

B-29's were used against the Japanese exclusively. Providing bases for their operation was one of the major reasons such islands as the Marianas were the object of costly, hard-won fighting by the Allies. It was from the Mariana Islands that Superfortresses began a systematic bombing offensive against Japan that exploited the concept of strategic air power to the full. More than 40 percent of the built-up areas in 66 Japanese cities were destroyed by the B-29. The bomber was partly responsible for defeating Japan and forcing her surrender without invasion.

The B-29 came into being as the result of USAAF specifications issued in December, 1939, for a "superbomber" to replace the B-17 and B-24. Once its design was approved, development and production were achieved fairly quickly.

The Superfortress raids on Japan—the first aerial attacks on the home islands since the Doolittle raid of April, 1942—commenced in June, 1944. By the beginning of August, 1945, these raids had reached massive proportions: more than 800 bombers a night, a total of nearly 160,000 tons of bombs dropped, huge areas of Tokyo gutted and flattened. Then, on August 6, a single B-29 named the "Enola Gay" dropped

The Boeing B-29 Superfortress was by far the largest major heavy bomber of the war. It was defended by four remote-controlled barbettes each with two or four .50 cal. machine guns and a direct-controlled tail turret containing two .50 cal. machine guns and a 20mm. cannon. It could carry 20,000 lb. of bombs.

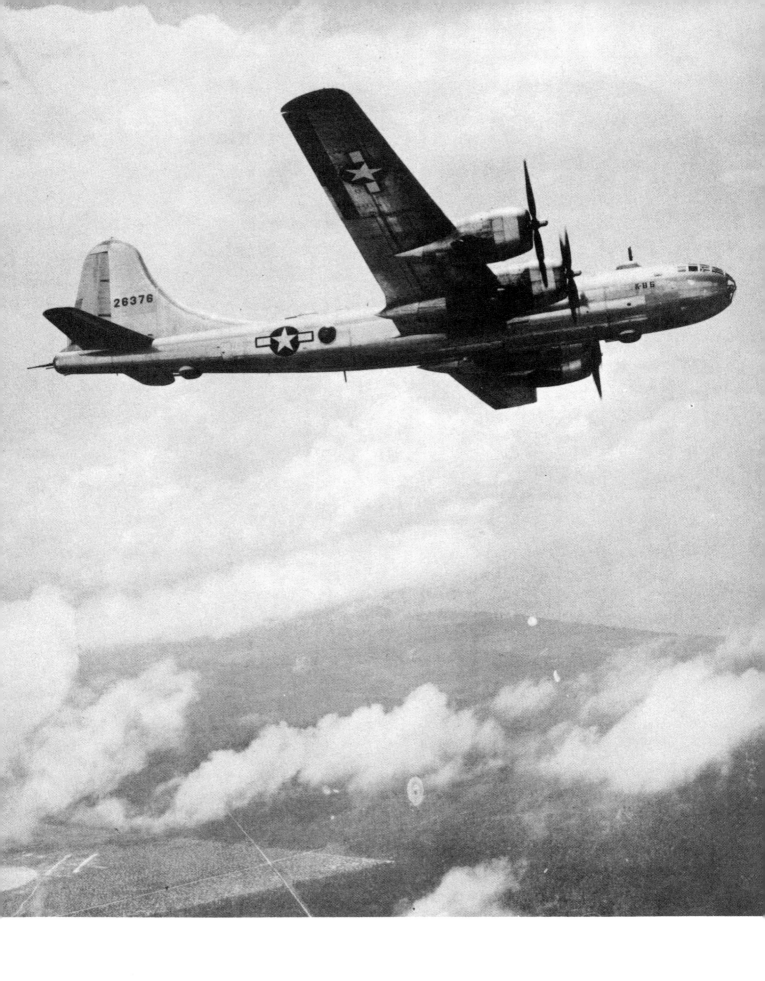

The B-29-45-MO (ser. 44-86292) "Enola Gay" was perhaps the single most famous bomber in history. For the Hiroshima raid all barbettes were removed and the standard tail insigne of the 393rd Bomber Squadron, to which the "Enola Gay" belonged, was replaced by a special arrow-and-circle device.

Hiroshima.

an atomic bomb on Hiroshima, and three days later, another B-29, "Bock's Car" dropped a second on Nagasaki.

The first bomb killed over 78,000 persons; the second, more than 73,000. The conventional raids had been more destructive, but there was a special kind of horror about the atomic bombing which the Japanese found insupportable. That 800 planes could destroy a city made a sort of dreadful sense; that a single plane could accomplish the same thing was unacceptable. The B-29's had delivered the weapon which ended the war, and they had been the handmaidens to the fearsome new age which was dawning.

TECHNICAL NOTES: The Boeing B-29 had four 2,200 h.p. Wright R-3350-23 air-cooled engines, a top speed of 357 m.p.h. at 30,000 ft., a span of 141.2 ft. and an armament of twelve .50 cal. machine guns and one 20mm. cannon and up to 20,000 lbs. of bombs for short ranges or 4,000 lbs. for long ranges.

The Oka Kamikaze

LIKE MOST AIRPLANES, THE JAPANESE OKA WAS AN AIR WEAPON especially created to do a particular job. It was a minute, 600 m.p.h. flying bomb, in every instance of use piloted by a dedicated warrior whose sworn intent was self-destruction at the greatest possible cost to the enemy. For the *Oka* rocket-propelled midget airplane was the ultimate means perfected to implement Japan's fantastic, horribly effective last-ditch concept of aerial warfare: *Kamikaze*.

The tactic was conceived and put into practice when it began to become apparent that Japan would lose the war. Once the attack method was evolved—early in 1944—17 special *Kamikaze* squadrons were formed within the army and navy air forces. Each unit consisted of twelve A6M Zero fighters equipped with two 500-lb. bombs. *Kamikaze* planes first saw action against the American fleet in Leyte Gulf. Their effect was devastating. Swooping down at dawn on October 14, 1944, thirty-five *Kamikaze* A6M's sank the cruiser *Houston*, three troopships, and inflicted crippling damage on the aircraft carriers *Hornet*, *Franklin* and *Hancock*. Thereafter, striking a naval convoy off Lingayen, they sank five ships, badly damaged twenty-five and injured another forty-two.

The initial success of the *Kamikaze* was impressive and terrifying. Naturally, their achievements made refinement of the tactic inevitable. The Zeros and Mitsubishi G4M bombers adapted for the practice were soon joined by the specially-created *Oka*. It made its debut in the battle for Okinawa, eighty-two days of brutal combat which began on April Fool's Day, 1945.

One of four **Oka** rocket-propelled suicide bombs found on Kadena Airfield, Okinawa. This version of the **Oka,** the MXY8, Mod. 11, was powered by three Type 4 rockets and carried a 2,200-lb. warhead. Some later models were jet-propelled.

A flaming Yokosuka (Aichi-produced) D4Y3 **Suisei** ("Judy") dive bomber attempts to crash-dive onto the flight deck of **Essex.**

Oka missiles were launched from "mother" planes such as this Mitsubishi G4M.

In the first order they received, *Kamikaze* pilots were instructed: "Choose a death which brings about the maximum result." At Okinawa, the order was expressly obeyed. Bomber-launched *Oka*'s and Zeros screamed down upon the mammoth naval force the United States had massed to take the tiny island. When the smoke of battle cleared, suicidal Japanese pilots had sunk 33 warships and 57 transports, damaged another 223 ships, killed 12,260 men and wounded 33,769. After the island was finally taken, hundreds of *Oka*'s were found stored in caves awaiting action. Luckily, American victory immobilized the potent weapons.

Kamikaze squadrons, however, continued to strike with ferocious effect from bases on the Japanese mainland. They attacked Okinawa daily. Even as the mushroom clouds rose above Nagasaki, *Kamikaze* craft, *Oka*'s and Kawanishi N1K fighters—were in the air and battle-bound. Four of the latter performed the last *Kamikaze* attack of the war. Together they dove into an explosive-laden American transport. The result produced a tidal wave.

When it is understood that *Kamikaze* pilots chose to die and were eager to do so, the tremendous potency of the bizarre air weapon is self-evident. Undeniably, the *Oka* and other forms of *Kamikaze* were one of the most destructive, successful air weapons devised and used in the war.

TECHNICAL NOTES: The Yoksuka (prime producer was Kasumigaura) MXY8 Oka, Mod. 11, was powered by three Type 4, Mk. I, Mod. 20 dry-fuel rockets each of 1,760 lbs. s.t. and carried a 2,200-lb. warhead. The later MXY8, Mod. 22 was powered by a TSU-11 jet engine of 440 lb. s.t.

The Gliders

THE TREATY OF VERSAILLES HAD PLACED STRICT LIMITATIONS ON THE development of German military aviation. As a result, much of Germany's pilot training prior to the mid-1930's was conducted in gliders and sail-planes. From this experience the Germans came to appreciate the potentialities of gliders as weapons of war.

After failing to cross the English Channel, Germany struck south and invaded Yugoslavia and Greece. She drove the British out of the Balkans, established airfields, and from them launched an invasion of Crete. After undergoing an intense and prolonged bombing attack, the British evacuated the bulk of their forces from the island at the end of April, 1941. The Germans undertook their invasion the next month. The first wave of the assault force arrived in gliders. Their use was the first to occur in World War II.

The gliders at Crete, made of wood covered with fabric, were DFS-230As. Each carried ten men and a pilot. As many as ten of these motorless airplanes were towed behind Junkers Ju 52 and Ju 86 tow planes. But their debut was not entirely successful. Many of the gliders were shot down and destroyed by British ground fire. It took conventionally carried paratroops and ship-ferried infantry to secure the invasion. The potential usefulness of gliders, however, was discounted neither by the Germans nor the Allies.

Following Crete, Germany introduced its large Gotha Go 242 glider. Drawn by the Junkers Ju 52 transport, it carried 25 men with

An American Waco CG-4A glider being towed off a British airfield by a C-47 transport. Like most military gliders the Waco was designed solely for towing; even unloaded it could not be used as a sail plane.

The Horsa (this one has USAAF markings and D-day stripes) was the RAF's most important glider. Larger than the Waco, it could carry 30 men.

The first military glider to see action was the German DFS 230A.

The huge German Messerschmitt Me 323 was converted from a glider to a six-engine transport.

full equipment. Gotha Go 242 gliders were used to airlift men and supplies to Rommel in North Africa.

The climax of German glider development was the enormous Messerschmitt Me 321. The craft had a wing-span of 181 feet and could carry a full military load of 40,000 lb. or 120 fully equipped troops. So bulky and unmanageable was the Me 321 that a powered variant called the Me 323 was quickly produced as a replacement. A number of these six-engine Me 323's were used to ferry troops and supplies to the besieged Afrika Korps in the closing days of the Tunisian campaign. Many were caught in the air by Allied fighters and the resulting slaughter prompted the Germans, thereafter, to use the great transports only sparingly.

The Allies quickly followed the German lead in military gliders. American airborne troops in Waco CG-4A's swooped down on Licata, Gela, Noto and Syracuse in Sicily while regular troops hit the beaches and paratroops rained down from the skies.

The Wacos were used again in the invasions of both northern and southern France. Along with larger British Horsas, vast numbers were employed in the unsuccessful airborne grab for the Rhine crossing at Arnheim in September, 1944—the last and greatest glider operation of the war.

TECHNICAL NOTES: The Waco CG-4A had a span of 83.6 ft. and could carry 13 fully armed troops. The Horsa had a span of 88 ft. and could carry 30 men. The Me 323 had a top speed of 190 m.p.h. and could carry 130 men or 18 tons of cargo.

SHIPS

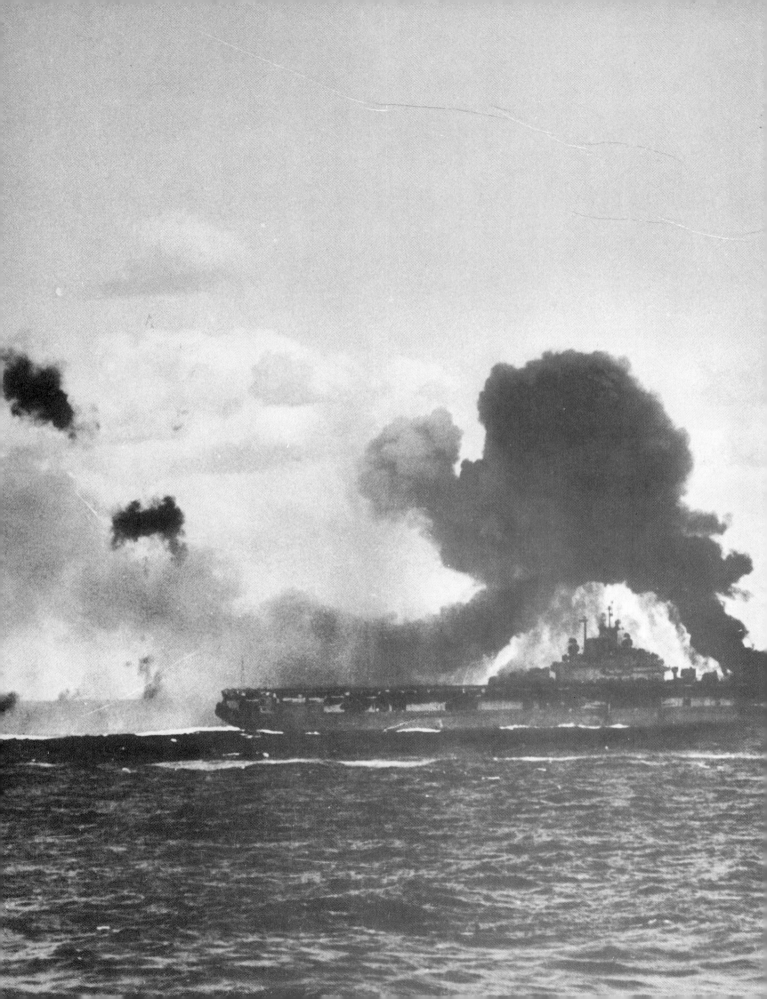

WARSHIPS ARE AT ONCE THE MOST COMPLEX AND INDIVIDUAL OF WEAPONS.
Each vessel is actually a congeries of weapons systems, yet each has an identity and a vitality which transcend the sum of its parts.

It is difficult to avoid the pathetic fallacy when writing of the great warships of World War II—to refrain from anecdotes, characterizations and even personifications of individual ships, and to concentrate on what was historically significant. Yet World War II was actually a pivotal time in the history of naval warfare.

It marked, for example, the technical climax and operational decline of the battleship, that great gun platform which, since before the days of Hawkins and Drake, had been the principal instrument for control of the seas. U.S.S. *Iowa*'s giant 16-inch 50 cal. rifles could hurl projectiles weighing well over a ton some 25 miles, but SBD's launched from the flight decks of *Essex* class carriers had combat radii of over 500 miles and could, among other things, sink battleships.

Nor was carrier aviation the only innovation in naval warfare. The submarine emerged, in the hands of the Germans and the Americans, as one of the most formidable weapons in the whole arsenal of war. Many experts felt, indeed, that it was the single most effective type of warship. The victory which the Allied antisubmarine campaign won in the Battle of the Atlantic, even though it made a major contribution to Germany's defeat, was, from the technological point of view, only temporary. Whether similar success could have been achieved in dealing with the type XXI boats which Germany was building at the end of the war is far from clear.

Still another innovation was the development of that complex of machines and techniques which make up amphibious warfare. Or, again, there is the still largely unevaluated question of mine warfare. And so on. The list is enormous and there is not space even to begin to cover it. We can do no more than remind ourselves, when we speak of the great ships of World War II, of the broader implications which underlay their individual exploits.

The Bismarck

THE GERMAN BATTLESHIP BISMARCK, ALONG WITH HER SISTER, TIRPITZ, was one of the most powerful warships ever launched. She displaced 42,000 tons, mounted a main battery of eight modern 15-inch guns, used one of the world's best optical fire-control systems and had an over-all watertight integrity which, in her last hours, made her seem nearly unsinkable. She was, as Winston Churchill said, "a masterpiece of naval construction."

Bismarck and *Tirpitz,* the smaller battleships *Scharnhorst* and *Gneisenau* and the three "pocket battleships" exemplified Germany's concept of the "fleet-in-being." According to this theory, the Germany heavy surface units were to be used primarily for hit-and-run raids on enemy shipping and were to avoid combat with what were almost sure to be larger British naval forces. The German ships thus spent most of their time in heavily defended ports within easy striking distance of the Atlantic and North Sea—Barents Sea convoy routes. Their mere presence constituted a perpetual threat which could only be countered by the diversion of whole fleets (and quantities of aircraft) to constant patrol of the areas through which the German battleships could gain access to the open sea. And such diversions tended to weaken British naval strength both in the Mediterranean and along the U-boat-ravaged mid-ocean supply lanes.

The best opportunity which the Royal Navy had for breaking the threat of the *Kriegsmarine*'s "fleet-in-being" was to catch the German

The super battleship **Bismarck** figured in one of the war's most dramatic sea hunts. But a case can be made for arguing that **Tirpitz, Bismarck**'s less famous sister, had a more significant over-all effect on Allied naval operations.

The **King George V** class battleships were among Britain's newest when the war began. They displaced 35,000 tons and carried ten 14-inch guns.

The 42,100-ton battle cruiser **Hood** was the Royal Navy's largest warship before it was sunk by **Bismarck** on May 24, 1941.

The German battleship **Scharnhorst** and its sister **Gneisenau** displaced 26,000 tons and carried nine 11-inch guns. **Scharnhorst** was sunk in a sea battle in December, 1943.

ships at sea when they sortied on raiding cruises. This was how the "pocket battleship" *Graf Spee* had been destroyed, and this, ultimately, was what happened to both *Bismarck* and *Scharnhorst*.

Bismarck made her last sortie from the harbor at Bergen, Norway, late in May, 1941. Accompanied by the cruiser *Prinz Eugen*, she soon encountered a British force led by the battleship *Prince of Wales* and the battle cruiser *Hood*, then the world's largest warship. In a brief exchange of salvoes *Bismarck* scored a lucky hit on *Hood* which exploded the battle cruiser's magazine and sent her to the bottom.

Bismarck's captain, knowing that the whole surface strength of Britain's Atlantic fleet would soon be in full pursuit, turned, and eluding the British under cover of fog, headed for Brest. With her great speed, *Bismarck* might have made good her escape. Unfortunately for the Germans, however, *Bismarck*'s position was located and on May 26 an attack from Swordfish torpedo planes damaged her steering gear and fatally reduced her speed. In due course a great collection of British naval might caught up with and surrounded the wounded German battleship. Fighting to the end, she endured a hail of major calibre shells and Swordfish-, destroyer- and cruiser-launched torpedoes. Finally, at 1101 on May 27, a torpedo spread launched from the cruiser *Dorsetshire* sent the monster to the bottom.

Tirpitz kept close to her Norwegian base, haunting the convoy routes to Russia. She gave a fearful demonstration of the "fleet-in being" tactic in the summer of 1942 when, simply by poking her bow out of her fjord, she drew off the entire heavy naval escort of convoy PQ-17. Left unprotected to the mercy of the *Luftwaffe* and the U-boats, 21 of PQ-17's 34 ships were sunk.

Scharnhorst was caught and sunk during a sortie late in 1943 and *Tirpitz* was destroyed by bombing the following year. Since most of Germany's other heavy surface units had also become inoperable from air attack, the threat of the "fleet-in-being" was at last dissipated.

TECHNICAL NOTES: Bismarck displaced 42,000 tons and measured 791 ft. at the water line. Armament included eight 15-inch, twelve 5.9-inch and sixteen 4.1-inch guns. Twin-shaft geared turbines gave 150,000 S.H.P. and a speed of 30 knots.

H.M.S. Warspite

H. M. S. WARSPITE WAS AMONG THE FIFTEEN BATTLESHIPS ON ACTIVE service with the Royal Navy when the war broke out in 1939. The group included *Hood, Rodney, Nelson, Queen Elizabeth* and *Valiant,* most of which had been laid down and completed prior to 1920. They were truly "old line." Nevertheless, their sturdiness and the fighting abilities of their fine crews enabled them to bridge the design gap separating them from more advanced ships possessed by the enemy.

The battle exploits of *Warspite* were typical of the great tradition Britain maintains in naval warfare. She was particularly instrumental in the destruction of the Italian fleet in the Mediterranean, where she was sent following successful action against German-held supply ports in Norway in the spring of 1940.

In March, 1941, *Warspite,* her battleship contemporaries *Barham* and *Valiant,* the aircraft carrier *Formidable,* four cruisers and twelve destroyers undertook an attack which desolated a large segment of the Italian fleet. Preceded by a vanguard of torpedo planes, the British task force caught an Italian squadron of eight cruisers, the redoubtable battle-ship *Vittorio Veneto* and a number of destroyers southeast of Cape Mata-pan in Greece. Torpedoes scored heavily against *Vittorio Veneto,* forcing her to limp away toward her base at Taranto. In short order, *Warspite, Barham* and *Valiant* closed on the cruiser *Fiume.* Their 15-inch guns pounded her to bits, then swung to deal the same killing blow to *Zara,* which broke apart. At the same time fire from other British ships sank the

The massive block-like superstructure of **Warspite** was typical of many British battleships. When this picture was taken, **Warspite** was carrying the flag of Sir James Somerville, Commander of the Eastern Fleet.

Nelson (above) and **Rodney** displaced about 33,900 tons and carried nine 16-inch guns in three turrets, all of which were set forward of the superstructure.

H.M.S. **Prince of Wales** was a **George V** class battleship. It was sunk by Japanese torpedo bombers on December 8, 1941.

cruiser *Pola*. Two Italian destroyers also succumbed to the guns of *Warspite* and her companions. "It was not a battle," said one Italian sailor, "it was a disaster."

Wide ranging in her duties, *Warspite* was part of the naval force which covered the evacuation of Crete in 1941 and later, in March, 1942, rushed to the Indian Ocean to meet the threat posed by the appearance of Japanese carriers off Ceylon. Returning to the "Med" in 1943, *Warspite* and her sister, *Valiant,* covered the Allied landing at Salerno with massive salvoes from their 15-inch guns. In November, 1944, it was *Warspite* which supplied a major share of the bombardment which enabled the British to capture Walcheren Island, the principal fortress blocking the capture of Antwerp.

Never entirely replaced by the newer *George V* class ships, the old British battleships served honorably throughout the war. *Warspite*, sturdy as ever, served on for a time after the cessation of hostilities until, at long last, it was regretfully decided that she should be scrapped.

TECHNICAL NOTES: Warspite **displaced 30,600 tons and measured 634 ft. (w.l.). Armament included eight 15-inch, eight 6-inch, eight 4-inch and four 3-lb. guns. Four-shaft geared turbines gave 80,000 S.H.P. and a speed of 24 knots. King George V displaced 35,000 tons, had ten 14-inch guns and a speed of 30 knots.**

U.S.S. Maryland

ON THE MORNING OF DECEMBER 7, 1941, A THRILLING ARRAY OF American naval might was assembled in Pearl Harbor's "Battleship Row." In a close line at anchor lay *Maryland, Oklahoma, Tennessee, West Virginia, Arizona* and *Nevada*. Slightly ahead, *California* was moored by herself. Across from these great ships, *Pennsylvania,* flagship of the U. S. Pacific Fleet, rested in drydock.

At 7:55 A.M., all were secure, powerful in aspect and potential. Five minutes later the Japanese attacked and hell and chaos engulfed the Hawaiian base. Mercilessly bombed and torpedoed, *Arizona* exploded, crumpled, and sank, never to rise again. Five torpedoes eventually sent *Oklahoma* heeling over. Torpedoed and set on fire, *California* was purposely flooded and sunk to save her magazines from exploding. Between the stricken *Oklahoma* and the shore, *Maryland* sustained considerable bomb damage, but remained afloat. *West Virginia* sank, slowly settling until her decks were awash. *Nevada* was able to get underway, but was beached after taking two torpedoes. *Tennessee* fared much the same as *Maryland*. *Pennsylvania* also suffered bomb damage, but did not sink.

Subsequently restored, *California, Maryland, West Virginia, Tennessee,* and *Pennsylvania* came back to take part in a resounding defeat of their enemies. In the Battle for Leyte Gulf, which finally erased Japanese naval power, they played spectacular roles in the Battle of Surigao Strait, one of the three major engagements into which the over-all action was divided.

Before Pearl Harbor, **Maryland** bore the familiar "basket" masts which characterized many of America's older battleships.

After Pearl Harbor **Maryland** and the other salvageable U. S. battleships were refitted and extensively modified.

Navy fire fighters desperately battle flames aboard **West Virginia** at Pearl Harbor.

IJN battleship **Yamashiro** as it appeared before the war.

The Battle of Surigao Strait ended an era in naval warfare. Fought late in October, 1944, it was the last engagement of capital ships in which the classic naval battle line was employed. Indeed, even before Surigao, airpower had made this type of surface engagement something of an anachronism.

In 1905, Japan's Admiral Togo had defeated a major Russian fleet by "crossing the 'T' "—bringing his line of ships and the fire of their guns across a vertical line of advance formed by the enemy. Whereas the ships forming the cross of the "T" could bring all their big guns to bear on the enemy line, the ships in the stem could only reply with fire from their forward turrets. This was the grand maneuvre successfully duplicated by the U. S. Navy against Togo's successors in Surigao Strait.

Into the strait, under cover of darkness, came the Japanese battleships *Fuso* and *Yamashiro,* four cruisers and a cluster of destroyers. Waiting for them at the other end of the strait were the five old U. S. battleships (plus *Mississippi*) and a large supporting force of cruisers, destroyers and PT boats under the overall command of Rear Admiral Jesse Oldendorf.

Fuso, Yamashiro, and a number of Japanese destroyers were badly mauled by torpedo attacks from U. S. destroyers and PT boats, but what was left of the Japanese force steamed steadily on to form the stem of Oldendorf's "T." The "T" was crossed, probably for the last time in history, at 3:51 A.M., October 24, 1944. A few hours later, the captain of the battered Japanese destroyer *Shigure* tersely radioed his superiors, "All ships except *Shigure* went down under gunfire and torpedo attack."

TECHNICAL NOTES: Maryland originally displaced 31,500 tons and measured 600 ft. (w.1.). Armament included eight 16-inch, sixteen 5-inch and many 40mm. and 20mm. guns. Four-shaft turbines with electric drive gave 27,300 S.H.P. and a speed of 21 knots.

U.S.S. Washington

U. S. S. WASHINGTON WAS THE SECOND BATTLESHIP TO BE COMPLETED and placed in service by the United States during the war. She was commissioned early in 1942, and with her sister ship *North Carolina* presaged that zenith of surface power achieved with the building of the world's most powerful battleships: *Iowa, Missouri, New Jersey* and *Wisconsin* in 1943–44.

Washington and *North Carolina* were the first major reinforcements supplied to the U. S. Navy following Pearl Harbor. They were soon supplemented by the battleships *Alabama, Indiana, Massachusetts* and *South Dakota.* All six played prominent parts in the war in the Pacific.

Washington performed with conspicuous effect during the final phase of the Naval Battle of Guadalcanal—an action which has been marked in modern history as one of the most desperately contested encounters between American and Japanese naval forces.

Major naval combat in the battle occurred November 12–15, 1942. On the night of November 12–13, five American cruisers with escorting destroyers engaged a large Japanese force led by the battleships *Hiei* and *Kirishima,* both of which had been part of the force which attacked Pearl Harbor. Grossly out-gunned, the American cruisers were shot to pieces—two sunk and two wrecked—but not before their guns and attacks by U. S. aircraft had so disabled *Hiei* that she was finally sunk. The remainder of the Japanese force, less some sinking destroyers, temporarily withdrew.

Washington and **North Carolina** were the first new battleships to join the U. S. Navy after World War II had begun. This picture gives a good idea of **Washington**'s powerful secondary battery of twenty 5-inch guns.

Iowa was the class leader of America's heaviest battleship class. Displacing 45,000 tons and armed with nine 16-inch guns, twenty 5-inch guns and 128 40mm. and 20mm. guns, she had a maximum trial speed of 32 kts.

A broad-beamed U. S. battleship opens up on Japanese shore installations on Okinawa.

They returned on the night of November 14–15, *Kirishima* leading two heavy cruisers, three light cruisers and ten destroyers. At first it seemed that the Americans would only be able to oppose this mighty force with destroyers and PT boats. Then, just as the U. S. PT screen was making first contact with the enemy, a cheery voice came up on the American radio sets. "This is Ching Chong China Lee . . . Get the hell out of the way; I'm coming through." It was RADM W. A. Lee, bringing *Washington* and *South Dakota* into battle. In the violent action which followed, *Washington*'s 16-inch guns pounded *Kirishima* into blazing scrap iron and left her sinking. The remainder of the Japanese force, having struck a quick murderous blow at the U. S. destroyers and having lost a cruiser and a destroyer of their own, fled. *Washington* had converted what might have been an American disaster into a clear-cut victory.

Yet despite their enormous power, the great victories they won and their strategic importance throughout the war, the days when battleships were the supreme weapons of naval war were past. In a sense, when the American battleships were bombed at Pearl Harbor, they and their counterparts in all the navies of the world were the permanent victims of airpower. From that time on it was the aircraft carrier with all the mobility, range and striking power implicit in its air weapon, which became the queen of battle at sea.

TECHNICAL NOTES: Washington displaced 35,000 tons and measured 704 ft. (w.l.). Armament included nine 6-inch, twenty 5-inch and seventy 40mm. and 20mm. guns. Four-shaft geared turbines gave 115,000 S.H.P. and a trial speed of 28 knots. Iowa displaced 45,000 tons, had nine 16-inch guns and a speed of 33 knots.

H.M.S. Illustrious

THROUGHOUT WORLD WAR II, THE IMPORTANCE OF AIR POWER MADE aircraft carriers indispensable participants in nearly all major sea battles fought both in the Atlantic and the Pacific. Britain was first (although perhaps not foremost) in developing carriers into vital weapons and employing them in major offensive operations. Her carrier force at the beginning of hostilities included *Illustrious, Formidable,* and *Victorious* —successors to her first modern carrier, the famous *Ark Royal.* It was planes from *Ark Royal* and *Victorious* which figured in the hunt and slaying of *Bismarck.* The destruction of the bulk of the French fleet in order to deprive Hitler of its use following the fall of France was in part the work of aircraft from *Ark Royal.*

The performance of *Illustrious* is typical of the effective use Britain made of her carriers. In the fall of 1940, she launched a bold attack upon the Italian fleet based at Taranto. On the night of November 11, wave after wave of Swordfish from *Illustrious* streaked into the air. The torpedo bombers penetrated a heavy anti-aircraft barrage and dashed in to put a major segment of the Italian navy out of action with one blow.

Six Italian battleships, five cruisers, and numerous destroyers were caught in the trap of their own harbor. The battleships *Littorio* and *Caio Duilio* were severely damaged and had to be beached to avoid sinking. The battleship *Conte di Cavour* went down, and a variety of cruisers and destroyers were blasted out of action. When *Illustrious* rejoined the fleet she had left to go it alone, flags fluttered from the fore-

Illustrious was the leader of Great Britain's largest and newest class of carriers when the war began. **Ark Royal** was slightly smaller and of a somewhat earlier design, but is generally grouped with the other three ships of the **Illustrious** class.

This picture, taken from the deck of **Illustrious,** shows **Indomitable,** leader of a newer post-1939 carrier class. **Illustrious** was at this time (1944) carrying the flag of RADM Sir Philip Vian, famed former captain of **Cossack.**

This recognition model shows the silhouette of the Italian battleship **Littorio,** victim of **Illustrious'** Swordfish at Taranto.

yards of the great British battleship *Warspite.* In classic British understatement they told her: "*Illustrious'* maneuvre well executed."

Following her overwhelming success at Taranto, *Illustrious* served with distinction shepherding an important Allied convoy to Malta. She suffered heavy damage from air attack, however, and was eventually impelled to seek respite and repair in the United States. The standard of superb action she set at Taranto was carried on by her sister ship, *Formidable,* at the Battle of Cape Matapan, when planes from *Formidable* combined with the firepower of a British battle fleet to drive the Italian surface Navy from the open waters of the Mediterranean.

TECHNICAL NOTES: Illustrious displaced 23,000 tons and measured 753 ft. (w.1.). She carried sixteen 4.5-inch and numerous 2-lb. pompom guns and about 35 aircraft. Three-shaft geared turbines gave 110,000 S.H.P. and a speed of 31 knots.

The Akagi

A FLEET OF 10 AIRCRAFT CARRIERS COMPRISED JAPAN'S FIRST LINE OF offense when she declared war upon the United States. Six of them, the heavy carriers, were the heart of the striking force which attacked Pearl Harbor. From their flight decks were launched the 360 torpedo and dive bombers, horizontal and high-level bombers and fighters which desolated the great mid-Pacific naval base.

Flagship of the striking force was the carrier *Akagi,* a converted battle cruiser. Her companion ships included *Kaga*—once a battleship, and *Shokaku, Zuikaku, Soryu* and *Hiryu.* They were guarded by the battleships *Hiei* and *Kirishima,* two heavy cruisers, a light cruiser, nine destroyers, and three submarines.

At 6:00 A.M. on the morning of December 7, 1941, all were poised on the brink of attack 230 miles north of Pearl Harbor. Aboard *Akagi,* Admiral Nagumo, in command of the raid, marked zero hour by hoisting the same flag—"Z," for attack—flown by Togo when he destroyed the Russian fleet at Tsushima, off Korea, in 1905. The sea was running high, but one by one the planes buzzed into the air from the long, flat flight decks of the carriers. The bombers and fighters circled, gathered in formation, and roared south. Their attack began at 7:55 A.M. It was all over slightly less than two hours later. All but 28 planes returned. By noon, the carriers and their escort were enroute back to the Japanese mainland. All on board were silent. The gravity of what had taken place—their overwhelming victory—left them sober and reflective.

Akagi was the best known ship in the three classes of heavy carriers which comprised the core of Admiral Nagumo's great First Air Fleet. About the only virtue of this dim pre-war photo is that it shows **Akagi's** odd downward-curving funnel.

The Japanese heavy carrier **Shokaku** was damaged in the Battle of the Coral Sea and consequently was unable to rejoin the Imperial Navy in time for the attack on Midway.

The heavy carrier **Lexington** was a casualty of the Battle of the Coral Sea which the U. S. could ill afford. This picture was taken shortly after the "abandon ship" order had been given.

Following Pearl Harbor, *Akagi* sailed home, but *Soryu* and *Hiryu*, accompanied by cruisers and destroyers, broke off their return to spearhead the invasion of Wake Atoll. In January and February, 1942, *Akagi* and three other carriers of the Nagumo Force struck targets in New Guinea and New Britain. By the end of February they were operating in support of the invasion of Java, where they sank nearly forty allied ships.

In March, the entire Force, less *Kaga,* burst into the Indian Ocean. Here they ran amok, bombing targets in Ceylon; shooting down quantities of British aircraft; and sinking the cruisers *Cornwall* and *Dorsetshire* (the same *Dorsetshire* which had delivered the *coup de grâce* to the superbattleship *Bismarck*) and the aircraft carrier *Hermes.*

In May, elements of the Nagumo Force tangled for the first time with American carriers in the Coral Sea. The encounter was expensive for both sides but it was a narrow tactical victory for Japan. *Shokaku* was damaged and the small carrier *Shoho* was sunk, but *Lexington* was also sunk and *Yorktown* badly damaged. Only three heavy U. S. carriers were left in the Pacific.

It had been a dazzling six months for the Imperial Navy's carriers. The Japanese could not know that in less than thirty more days, two-thirds of the Nagumo Force would be at the bottom of the Pacific Ocean.

TECHNICAL NOTES: Akagi and Kaga displaced 27,000 tons and measured 750 ft. (w.1.). They carried ten 8-inch guns and about 65 aircraft. Shokaku and Zuikaku displaced 20,000 tons; Hiryu and Soryu, 10,050 tons.

U.S.S. Enterprise

THE HEAVY AIRCRAFT CARRIERS POSSESSED BY THE UNITED STATES WHEN the war in the Pacific broke out were *Wasp, Hornet, Yorktown, Saratoga, Lexington* and *Enterprise*. The latter three were on duty with the Pacific Fleet when Pearl Harbor was attacked. *Enterprise* was only 200 miles from Oahu but missed the raid. *Lexington* was at sea, and *Saratoga* about to dock in San Diego. All were ordered to Pearl Harbor. Before the year was out they were cruising the waters west of Honolulu seeking the enemy. They were shortly joined by *Hornet* and *Yorktown*. Fast carrier striking forces were organized and operations against enemy-held island bases got underway. *Saratoga* headed for Wake Atoll to assist the embattled forces there. Before she could get into action, she was torpedoed by an enemy submarine on January 11, 1942. She survived, but was out of service for months.

In the months that followed, *Lexington, Enterprise, Hornet* and *Yorktown* pressed the attack upon the Japanese in the South Pacific. In April, *Hornet* made history by launching the famous flight of B-25 Mitchell bombers which struck Tokyo, Nagoya, Osaka, and Kobe. *Lexington* and *Yorktown* engaged the enemy in the Coral Sea, where things came to a head early in May.

The Battle of the Coral Sea marked the end of the Japanese thrust into the South Pacific. It may have saved Australia from invasion and it certainly helped to focus Japanese attention on the problem of destroying the U. S. carriers—a preoccupation which led to Midway. But at the time, the Coral Sea seemed a clear-cut victory to the Japanese.

Enterprise, along with the twice-torpedoed **Saratoga,** was the only one of the original Pacific Fleet heavy carriers to survive the first year of the Pacific war.

The Japanese light carrier **Shoho** was sunk by U. S. Navy aircraft in the Battle of the Coral Sea.

Yorktown, heavily damaged in the Battle of the Coral Sea, was quickly repaired at Pearl Harbor and joined **Enterprise** and **Hornet** in the decisive Battle of Midway.

The Battle of the Coral Sea was the first all-carrier duel in history, and it was an expensive first for the U. S. Navy. The old *Lexington*, "queen of the flattops," was wrecked by Japanese bombs and torpedoes. The order to abandon ship was given and destroyer *Phelps* set about sinking the carrier. "I couldn't watch her go," said a survivor, "and men who had been with her since she was commissioned in '27 stood with tears streaming."

Yorktown had also been badly hit in the Coral Sea. Damage Control estimated that it would take ninety days at Pearl Harbor to bring the ship back to a condition of operational readiness. But the Navy could not afford ninety days. Intelligence had learned that a massive Japanese fleet was preparing to attack Midway in less than a month.

When *Yorktown* reached Pearl Harbor, repair parties swarmed aboard her and, working round the clock, put her back in fighting trim in the miraculous time of forty-eight hours. Thus *Yorktown* was able to join *Enterprise* and *Hornet* in the decisive Battle of Midway where the Japanese carrier fleet was dealt a fatal blow.

By the end of 1942, *Lexington, Yorktown, Hornet* and *Wasp* had all been sunk, and *Saratoga* had again been put out of action by enemy torpedoes. But *Enterprise*, "the big 'E,' " led a charmed life. She was involved in many more savage battles, but survived to the end of the war, a worthy representative of that gallant group of carriers which had been America's first—and for all practical purposes, only—line of defense at sea during the terrible months which followed Pearl Harbor.

TECHNICAL NOTES: Enterprise **displaced 19,800 tons and measured 761 ft. (w.1.). Armament was eight 5-inch and many 40mm. and 20mm. guns and about 70 aircraft. Geared turbines gave 120,000 S.H.P. and a speed of 34 knots.**

The Essex Class Carriers

AMONG THE AIRCRAFT CARRIERS ALREADY SERVING WITH THE U. S. NAVY when the Pacific war began, few survived the first full year of hostilities. But while they fought, numerous successors were being built. By the close of 1943, a majority of the *Essex* class carriers authorized in 1940 were completed and in action southwest of Pearl Harbor. These included *Essex, Randolph, Intrepid* and *Bunker Hill;* and a new *Lexington, Yorktown, Hornet* and *Wasp.* The following year, as the American war effort got into stride, they were joined by others like *Franklin, Ticonderoga, Hancock* and a host of light and escort carriers.

United States carrier might swelled to mammoth proportions. The great fleet of fast carriers taught the enemy the lesson of Midway again and again. Carriers had become the most important capital ships in the Navy.

At Rabaul, in November, 1943, *Saratoga, Essex, Bunker Hill* and light carrier *Independence* clouded the sky with fighters, dive bombers, and torpedo bombers. Their combined force of planes destroyed 50 percent of Rabaul's fighters and 90 percent of its bombers.

From Rabaul, the long push north that culminated in the greatest sea-air battle in history—the Battle of Okinawa (April, 1945)—began. With *Saratoga* and *Enterprise, Yorktown, Lexington, Essex* and *Bunker Hill* launched strikes in the Gilberts in November, 1943. Then, replacing *Lexington, Intrepid* joined the same group in battering the Marshalls in early 1944. The air assault on Truk followed in February. Planes from

U.S.S. **Essex,** leader of America's largest war-time carrier class, being hit forward of No. 2 elevator by a Japanese **Kamikaze.**

The Japanese light carrier **Zuiho** was one of several sunk by air-craft from **Essex** class carriers during the Battle of Leyte Gulf.

This line-up of **Essex** class carriers and other heavy surface units suggests the magnitude of American naval power in the final year of the war.

A **Kamikaze** narrowly misses an **Independence** class light carrier.

Yorktown, Essex, Intrepid, Bunker Hill and *Enterprise* battered the enemy installation and its air strength insensible. The Japanese lost more than 265 planes and 32 ships.

Then, in June, 1944, a major naval engagement occurred some ninety miles off Saipan and Guam in the Marianas. Fifteen American carriers and seven battleships, their route scouted by submarines, engaged nine Japanese carriers and five battleships in a savage, all-out combat now called the Battle of the Philippine Sea. The planes of the American carriers stripped enemy air power raw in what was promptly dubbed "the Marianas turkey-shoot." The Japanese lost 402 planes. At sea-level, American submarines sank the carriers *Shokaku, Hiyo* and *Taiho*—a new flat-top and then the largest in the world. Other enemy carriers were severely damaged. Among them was *Zuikaku,* at the battle's end the last of the original force of carriers which sent their planes to Pearl Harbor. She survived until the Battle of Leyte Gulf, when planes from *Lexington, Essex* and *Intrepid* sank her.

By the end of the war the *Essex* class carriers and their numerous light and escort carrier colleagues composed far and away the world's largest carrier fleet. They had fought, and resoundingly won, the first carrier war in history. In all likelihood, it was also the last.

TECHNICAL NOTES: Essex class ships generally displaced 27,100 tons and measured 820 ft. (w.1.). Armament included eight 5-inch and many 40mm. and 20mm. guns. Four-shaft geared turbines gave 150,000 S.H.P. and a speed of 33 knots. Aircraft: between 75 and 100.

U.S.S. San Francisco

AMERICAN CRUISERS, HEAVY AND LIGHT, WERE INVOLVED IN SO MANY naval actions in World War II that it is difficult to describe adequately, in limited space, the vital role they played. But it was perhaps during the grueling campaign in the Solomons that those fast, powerful ships performed their most important services for their country.

A particularly heavy burden fell on the U. S. heavy cruisers during the period between August, 1942 and February, 1943, when American troops were struggling to make good their invasion of Guadalcanal. The naval war began within days of the Marines' initial landing on the island. At the Naval Battle of Savo Island, on August 8–9, a Japanese naval force surprised a smaller Allied force and in a few hellish minutes sent the cruisers *Vincennes, Astoria, Quincy* and H.M.A.S. *Canberra* to the bottom. This marked the grim beginning of what was to be a protracted series of some of the most savage naval battles in history.

Early in October, at the Battle of Cape Esperance, the heavy cruisers *San Francisco* and *Salt Lake City,* with the light cruisers *Helena* and *Boise,* mauled and were mauled by a similar Japanese force. Later the same month, *San Francisco* and others were present at the disastrous Battle of Santa Cruz Island which cost the United States the carrier *Hornet.*

In early November, carrying the flag of RADM Daniel Callaghan, *San Francisco,* with the heavy cruiser *Portland* and the light cruisers *Helena, Atlanta* and *Juneau,* took on a large Japanese force led by two

U.S.S. **San Francisco** as she looked on October 27, 1944, steaming into Pearl Harbor. Battered parts taken from **San Francisco** after the Naval Battle of Guadalcanal are still preserved by the city of San Francisco.

U.S.S. **Portland** was a veteran of twenty major Pacific operations between the Battle of the Coral Sea and VJ-day. Like **San Francisco** she was badly damaged at the Naval Battle of Guadalcanal.

At the Battle of Tassaforanga during the Solomons campaign, **Minneapolis** was torpedoed and set afire. She returned from repairs to take part in nearly every major Pacific action after October, 1943.

Baltimore led a large class of U. S. heavy cruisers built during the war. She carried nine 8-inch guns and twelve 5-inch guns.

battleships. Hopelessly outgunned, the U. S. cruisers suffered bitterly. When the smoke of forty-five minutes fighting cleared, *Atlanta* was an unsalvageable wreck, *Portland* was disabled and under tow and *Juneau*'s back was broken (she was shortly torpedoed and sunk). *San Francisco* had taken forty-five hits—all at point-blank range, many from 14-inch shells. She was a wreck above the water-line and twenty-two separate fires blazed on her decks. Admiral Callaghan and most of his staff were dead. Yet *San Francisco* somehow got under way and safely cleared the area under her own power.

Before the end of the month, the American heavy cruisers were involved in yet another punishing battle. At Tassafaronga *Minneapolis* was hit by two torpedoes, *New Orleans'* bow was blown away, *Pensacola* was set afire and *Northampton* was put out of action by two torpedo hits and fire in her fuel tanks.

By the end of the Guadalcanal Campaign in February, 1943, the United States had lost five heavy cruisers and well as two carriers, two light cruisers, and fifteen destroyers. The Japanese had lost two battleships, a carrier, four cruisers, and twelve destroyers. The attrition had been intensely painful to both sides, but it was an attrition which the Americans could afford and the Japanese could not. The sacrifices of the U. S. Navymen at Guadalcanal had not been made in vain, for the Japanese surface fleet was never able to replace the losses it had sustained during the campaign.

TECHNICAL NOTES: San Francisco displaced 9,950 tons and measured 574 ft. (w.1.). Armament was nine 8-inch, twelve 5-inch and numerous smaller guns. Four-shaft geared turbines gave 107,000 S.H.P. and a speed of 32.7 knots.

U. S. S. Cleveland

ON THE NIGHT OF FEBRUARY 1, 1943, THE JAPANESE, AT LONG LAST,
began their evacuation of Guadalcanal. The Guadalcanal Campaign had
decimated the American heavy cruiser forces and it was therefore left
primarily to the light cruisers and destroyers to carry the burden of surface action during the subsequent American sweep north through the
central Solomons to Bougainville.

Not, to be sure, that the light cruisers had previously been strangers
to battle. *Helena* had been through Cape Esperance, Santa Cruz, and the
Naval Battle of Guadalcanal. *Boise,* at Cape Esperance, had taken nearly
as much punishment as did *San Francisco* a month later off Guadalcanal,
where the light cruisers *Atlanta* and *Juneau* were sunk.

The first major naval action of the second phase of the Solomons
Campaign occurred on July 6, 1943. Returning from a shore bombardment in support of the American invasion of New Georgia, light cruisers
Helena, Honolulu and *St. Louis* intercepted a fast "Tokyo Express" at-
tempting to reinforce New Georgia. In the ensuing battle the Japanese
convoy was broken up but the gallant *Helena* was torpedoed and sunk.

Less than a week later, in another bitter encounter with a "Tokyo
Express," *Honolulu, St. Louis* and H.M.N.Z.S. *Leander* (sister to *Ajax*
and *Achilles* which hounded *Graf Spee* to its doom) were all severely
damaged. American cruiser strength in the Solomons had nearly been
wiped out. For the remainder of the summer, the task of combatting the
Japanese naval forces in the area was carried out almost entirely by
destroyers.

U.S.S. **Denver** was one of the **Cleveland** class cruisers under
Admiral Merrill's command at the major Naval Battle of Empress
Augusta Bay, fought off Bougainville on November 2, 1943.

132

The **Brooklyn** class cruisers were pre-war designs. **Honolulu,** **Boise** and **Phoenix** (above) belonged to this class.

Atlanta and **Juneau,** lost at the Naval Battle of Guadalcanal, belonged to the new **Oakland** class. The **Oakland's** main armament consisted of twelve or sixteen 5-inch guns.

But reinforcements were on the way. Units of the new *Cleveland* class—soon to become the world's most numerous light cruiser class—began to arrive in the Solomons. By October, when the Americans landed on Bougainville, RADM "Tip" Merrill had at his disposal *Cleveland, Montpelier* (flagship), *Columbia* and *Denver* as well as the veteran destroyers of Captain Arleigh Burke's DesDiv 45 and the recently arrived DesDiv 46. The stage was set for the last of the great Solomons naval battles, Empress Augusta Bay.

In the small hours of the morning of November 2, Merrill's ships encountered a Japanese force of two heavy cruisers, two light cruisers, and six destroyers bent on knocking out the Bougainville beachhead. The action which followed was described by Merrill as "organized hell." It was certainly this for the Japanese. Not only did they fail to accomplish their mission, but almost their whole force sustained major damage and the cruiser *Sendai* and a destroyer were sunk.

With the loss of Bougainville, the Japanese had lost the Solomons. This, in turn, meant that the major Japanese base at Rabaul had been outflanked and that the Japanese war effort in the South Pacific had been all but paralyzed.

TECHNICAL NOTES: Cleveland displaced 10,000 tons and measured 614 ft. (w.l.). Armament included twelve 6-inch, twelve 5-inch and many 40mm. and 20mm. guns. Four-shaft geared turbines gave 120,000 S.H.P. and a speed of 33 knots.

H.M.S. Ajax

HEAVY AND LIGHT CRUISERS OF ALL THE COMBATANTS PLAYED IMportant roles in every area of naval action. The light cruisers of Britain in particular earned fame in the early stages of the war: *Ajax* and *Achilles* which joined the heavy cruiser *Exeter* in the fight with the German battleship *Admiral Graf Spee* off Montevideo; *Orion, Ajax, Perth* and *Gloucester* which helped in the defeat of a major segment of the Italian fleet in the Battle of Cape Matapan; *Dido, Euryalus* and *Cleopatra* in the relief and re-enforcement of Malta. The performance of these ships exemplified the abilities of their type: good cruising range, high speed, and amazing fighting power.

Two months after hostilities began in Europe British light cruisers were deployed in every part of the world. The *Graf Spee* encounter initiated their reputation for winning against odds. The German battleship was on a raiding cruise in the south Atlantic. The task of destroying her fell to *Ajax, Achilles* and *Exeter,* any of which she could pound to pieces with her 11-inch guns without coming in range of their less powerful armament. Nevertheless, the three cruisers hunted *Graf Spee* down and closed to attack shortly after dawn, December 13, 1939, off the coast of Uruguay. In the gun-duel which followed, *Exeter* was badly wounded, but inflicted enough damage on *Graf Spee* to make her retreat. *Exeter* broke off fighting while *Ajax* and *Achilles* took up the chase. Despite the danger, the two steamed within five miles of the *Graf Spee*'s guns and renewed the fight. Faster and more nimble than the *Graf Spee,*

The veteran British light cruiser **Ajax** (above), with her sister **Achilles,** and the heavy cruiser **Exeter,** hunted down the German pocket battleship **Graf Spee.**

Two **Dido** class light cruisers steam at high speed through the Mediterranean. The **Dido** ships displaced 5,450 tons and carried ten 5.25-inch guns.

The German pocket battleships were, in effect, battle cruisers. They displaced 10,000 tons and carried six 11-inch guns.

they scored hit upon hit as their larger opponent fled toward the neutral port of Montevideo in the mouth of the River Plate.

Graf Spee successfully reached refuge at nightfall. The cruisers took up watch outside. Seventy-two hours later the cornered battleship emerged, but not to renew the fight. She steamed slowly southwest as the commander of *Ajax* signalled: "My object—destruction." The cruiser launched her airplane to check the enemy's movements. There was no need; *Ajax* and *Achilles* had won the battle. Captain Langsdorff of *Graf Spee* had his crew removed to a German merchantman in Montevideo harbor. Upon reaching the open sea, he scuttled the giant. The next day, Captain Langsdorff shot himself.

From the south Atlantic, *Ajax* went to the Mediterranean. There she joined her sister ship *Orion* and others of her type in harrassing enemy coastal installations in North Africa, defeating the Italians at Matapan, and implementing the evacuation of Crete.

TECHNICAL NOTES: Ajax displaced 6,985 tons and measured 522 ft. (p.p.). Armament included eight 6-inch, eight 4-inch, four 3-lb. and numerous smaller guns, and eight 21-inch torpedo tubes. Four-shaft geared turbines gave 72,000 S.H.P. and a speed of 32.5 knots.

The Fletcher Class Destroyers

EVERY TYPE OF WARSHIP HAS ITS PARTISANS. OLD SALTS WILL confidently tell recruits that this or that kind of ship is "good duty." But destroyermen have a special boast. "Serve on a destroyer," they will say, "if you want to find out what the Navy is really all about."

There is more than a little justice in this. Destroyers can perform—on a scale appropriate to their size—the same combat functions as any larger warship, aircraft carriers excepted. Yet they are small enough so that every crewman can acquire a good working knowledge of the duties of all the ship's departments. Perhaps this helps to explain the intense loyalty that so many destroyermen feel towards their ships.

The United States had at least nine major classes of destroyers when the war began, and these were quickly supplemented by what was to become numerically the largest of the wartime destroyer classes, the *Fletcher*. Towards the end of the war, an even newer class, the superlative *Sumner* ships, began to join the fleet. At one point during the war, over 600 U. S. destroyers were in commission. In the Atlantic and Mediterranean they hunted submarines, guarded convoys and supported landings in Africa, Sicily, Italy and France. In the Pacific, where most of the U. S. fleet operated, they did just about everything.

The accounts of action seen by U. S. destroyers are legion, and the present volume can do no more than summarize a few representative examples. At the Battle of Surigao Strait, for example, in the preliminary engagement fought on the night of October 24, 1944, American de-

U.S.S. **Fletcher** led the largest American war-time destroyer class. The **Fletcher** ships carried their 5-inch guns in single mounts, two forward and three aft.

One-stack designs were typical of U. S. destroyer construction during the 1930's. U.S.S. **Patterson** (above) was a **Gridley** class ship.

The **Sumner** class destroyers, all built during the war, carried their six 5-inch guns in three twin mounts.

stroyers played an even more effective role than the battleships which later crossed the Japanese "T." Destroyers *McDermot, Monssen, Melvin, Killen, Hutchins, Newcomb,* and others scored devastating torpedo and gunfire hits on the Japanese battleships *Yamashiro* and *Fuso,* and the destroyers *Yamagumo, Michishio* and *Asagumo.* Admiral Nishimura's battle fleet was, in fact, in ruins even before it came under the guns of the American battleships.

In the Battle of Samar, October 25, 1944, destroyers *Heerman* (*Fletcher* class), *Hoel* and *Johnston* (*Gearing* class), along with destroyer escorts *Butler, Dennis, Raymond* and *Roberts* valiantly attempted to cover the retreat of six CVE's in the face of an overwhelming Japanese force of four battleships, eight cruisers and eleven destroyers. Of the U. S. destroyers, only *Heerman* survived the ensuing storm of 8-, 16-, and 18-inch Japanese shells. But the rearguard defense had been successful; only one CVE was lost.

Even though very lightly armored, destroyers could be remarkably hardy. At Okinawa *Laffey* (*Sumner* class) was subjected to twenty-two *Kamikaze* attacks in eighty minutes. Hit thirteen times, she not only survived but destroyed nine enemy aircraft in the bargain.

TECHNICAL NOTES: Fletcher class ships usually displaced 2,700 tons and measured about 400 ft. Armament included five 5-inch, four 40mm. and four 20mm. guns, and ten 21-inch torpedo tubes. Speed was 38 knots.

The Tribal Class Destroyers

BRITAIN'S ROYAL NAVY, WHEN WAR WAS DECLARED ON GERMANY IN THE fall of 1939, possessed 180 destroyers grouped into 28 classes. Some were two to three years old; many dated from the 1920s, and at least a dozen had begun their careers during World War I. To these, construction added another 150. An additional 50 were acquired from the United States in return for naval base concessions.

The number of Royal Navy destroyers lost during the war symbolizes the extreme demand British naval operations put upon these small, swift ships. No fewer than 148 succumbed in action. The bitter sea-fighting in the Atlantic, Mediterranean and North Sea during the initial years of conflict accounted for many.

Among Britain's numerous destroyer classes, the performance of the ships of the Tribal, *Javelin* and *Gallant* classes were representative. Their exploits embraced almost every form of naval action.

At the climax of the pursuit of *Bismarck,* Tribal class destroyers *Cossack, Maori, Sikh* and *Zulu* boldly closed on the gigantic battleship. They carried out a torpedo attack at point-blank range, well within the reach of their enemy's great guns. Torpedoes from *Cossack* and *Maori* marked the beginning of *Bismarck*'s end. For *Cossack,* it was all in a day's work. More than a year before she had established her reputation with a mission that recalled the days of the buccaneers. Under cover of night in February, 1940, *Cossack* slipped to the side of the German tanker *Altmark,* at anchor in Josing Fjord, Norway. A raiding party

H.M.S. **Tartar** became the Tribal class leader after **Cossack** was sunk. Ten of the original 16 **Tribal** destroyers had been lost by the beginning of 1944.

144

A **Javelin** class destroyer with a bone in her teeth. The **Javelin** ships displaced 1,690 tons and carried six 4.7-inch guns and five 21-inch torpedo tubes.

The **Mahratta** (later **Milne**) class destroyers were post-Tribal constructions. They carried their six 4.7-inch guns in three twin mounts.

H.M.S. **Cossack,** the original leader of the Tribal class. Probably the most famous British destroyer of World War II.

from the destroyer held the tanker's crew at bay and rescued some 300 British seamen—prisoners transferred to *Altmark* from the pocket battleship *Graf Spee* after she had returned from savaging British merchantmen in the South Atlantic.

Later that same spring, on April 13, while *Warspite* bombarded shore installations, Captain Vian of *Cossack* led a group of Tribal and other destroyers into Narvik Fjord. There, in a brief, violent action, they sank four German destroyers and two transports.

In the Mediterranean, Tribal destroyers *Mohawk* and *Nubian* assisted *Jervis* and *Janus* (*Javelin* class) in wrecking an enemy convoy bound for Tripoli. *Mohawk* was sunk by torpedoes during the engagement and her crew, bobbing about in the seething water, blithely chorused "Roll Out the Barrel" until they were rescued.

Javelin, Gallant, "S" and "H" class destroyers, played major roles at Matapan. "D" class *Dainty* later scored a Mediterranean record by sinking three Italian submarines in a single afternoon. And, characteristically, a Tribal ship, *Arunta,* even participated in that greatest of U. S. naval engagements, the Battle of Leyte Gulf.

TECHNICAL NOTES: Tribal ships displaced 1,870 tons and measured 355 ft. (w.l.). Armament included six 4.7-inch, two 4-inch and several smaller guns, and four 21-inch torpedo tubes. Speed was 36.5 knots.

The German U-Boats

"THE ONLY THING," WROTE WINSTON CHURCHILL IN *THEIR FINEST HOUR*, "that ever really frightened me during the war was the U-boat peril." And well it might. Germany's great submarine offensive was aimed, quite simply, at strangling England to death; and for a time, it seemed that Germany would succeed. The conduct of the U-boat operations was inspired, overwhelming, incredibly effective. In the Atlantic, the Channel, the North Sea and the Mediterranean, U-boats sank a fantastic total of 14.7 million tons of Allied merchant shipping. In addition, they destroyed 158 British warships, 29 American warships and quantities of aircraft.

When the war began, Germany possessed only 22 U-boats large enough for long-range operations, but new construction progressed rapidly, and by late 1942, the Germans were able to operate approximately 100 boats simultaneously in the Atlantic. During the early months of the war, the U-boats fueled and took on supplies from tankers cruising off the main trade routes. When the tankers were hunted down by the Royal Navy, the Germans designed special refueling submarines which eluded detection. At about the same time, the "wolf-pack" method of attack was developed. At first the U-boats attacked convoys in small groups of two or three, but in time the packs grew to relatively enormous proportions, sometimes numbering as many as 50 boats.

Germany developed a variety of ocean going U-boat types. Perhaps the most familiar and successful of the mid-war boats were the 740-ton

This 740-ton Type IXc U-boat was surrendered to U. S. troops at Bremerhaven in 1945. The forward deck gun was removed from most of the later German ocean-going submarines.

These deadly Type XXI boats were under construction at Bremen when the war ended.

A British convoy under attack. The destroyer in the foreground is Tribal class **Eskimo.**

A Type IX boat under air attack from a Grumman TBF.

Type IXc and the 1,600-ton Type XVI. The formidable IXc had a 15,000 mile cruising range, good torpedo capacity and excellent surface and submerged speeds.

Slaughter of Allied shipping reached a crescendo in June, 1942, when 190 ships were sunk, 69 of them in the Caribbean and the Gulf of Mexico. "Our submarines," boasted Admiral Dönitz, "are operating so close inshore along the American coast that bathers and sometimes whole cities are witnesses to that drama of war whose visual climaxes are the red glorioles of blazing tankers."

But the Allies had not been idle. New instruments and new techniques were slowly being brought to bear on the U-boat problem. New detection devices—radar, improved hydrophones and electronic echo-ranging gear—and new ASW ships and planes—jeep carriers, modified destroyers, ASW escort vessels, small craft and patrol aircraft—all began to take their toll of the German undersea fleet. By the summer of 1943, the U-boat loss-rate became unacceptable to Germany and the submarines were temporarily withdrawn from combat.

In 1944 Dönitz made another major effort to gain supremacy in the Atlantic. The important technical elements in this renewed campaign were the *Schnorkel,* an underwater breathing device for diesel engines, which permitted standard U-boats to run submerged for much longer periods, and the new 1,600-ton Type XXI boat which could run at 18 knots submerged and dive to the astounding depth of 700 feet. Despite intensive air raids on German shipyards and U-boat pens, more U-boats were produced in November, 1944, than any previous month of the war. But no clear-cut decision as to whether the new German weapons could overcome the Allies' anti-submarine techniques was reached. The collapse of Germany intervened. About 60 or 70 U-boats were still operating when the war ended.

TECHNICAL NOTES: The standard oceangoing Type IX displaced 740 tons and measured 244.5 ft. During the early part of the war one 4.1-inch deck gun was carried but this was later replaced by 37mm. and 20mm. guns. Six 21-inch torpedo tubes were mounted (4 bow; 2 stern). Surface speed was 18.5 knots. The Type XXI displaced 1,600 tons and had a submerged speed of 18 knots.

The Escort Carriers

IT BECAME APPARENT, EVEN IN THE EARLY MONTHS OF THE WAR, THAT the airplane was an exceptionally potent anti-submarine weapon. But the problem was how to provide continuous air cover to convoys in mid-ocean. There were few available planes with sufficient range to patrol the whole route or—even if they had the range—to stay on station for an adequate length of time.

One early British experiment designed to cope with the problem involved the use of so-called C. A. M. S. ships. These were freighters converted to carry a single aircraft which could be catapult-launched—but not recovered—in time of need. The C. A. M. S. ships had some success against German long-range patrol planes but little direct effect on the U-boats.

The real break-through came with the development of the escort carriers. The first American escort carriers (CVE's) were also converted oilers and C-3 freighters, but they were genuine—if miniature—flat-tops which carried a respectable complement of recoverable aircraft. Used initially for convoy duty, the CVE's proved so effective that they were soon assigned to cooperate with destroyers in small free-ranging task forces called "hunter-killer" teams. In December, 1943, U.S.S. *Bogue* and four destroyers sank U-172 in an action which was to be the prototype of all the hunter-killer operations which followed.

The Royal Navy also made extensive use of escort carriers. Early in the war the British had employed some of their few available light

The U. S. Escort Carrier **Guadalcanal**, DE's and TBF's circle the captured German U-505.

U.S.S. **Bogue** was one of the first CVE's to sink a U-boat while acting with a hunter-killer team.

H.M.S. **Battler** was typical of British CVE's.

carriers for escort duty, but true CVE types did not begin to arrive in the fleet until 1942. The British CVE's closely resembled their American counterparts and, indeed, many were built in American shipyards. One British type, the MAC ships, actually doubled in use, serving simultaneously as cargo carriers and aircraft carriers.

As the war progressed America's already large fleet of converted CVE's was supplemented by new escort carriers designed and built *ab initio* for the job which they were intended to perform. One of these new "jeep carriers," U.S.S. *Guadalcanal,* was involved in a notable incident which occurred off the coast of Africa in June, 1944.

Guadalcanal and five destroyer escorts made a sound contact with a U-boat at 1110 on June 4. TBF's from *Guadalcanal* were launched and strafed the U-boat as it ran at shallow depth beneath the surface. Minutes later, after a DE had straddled the submarine with depth charges, the German commander surfaced. Caught in a crossfire from the DE's and circling aircraft, the U-boat's crew abandoned ship so hastily that they did not take time to sink her. Thus, for the first time in 129 years, the U. S. Navy had captured an enemy warship in combat. For this action, *Guadalcanal* and its team were awarded the Presidential Unit Citation. *Guadalcanal*'s commander was, incidentally, Captain Daniel V. Gallery—now an Admiral and a best-selling author.

TECHNICAL NOTES: Most U. S. CVE's 9,000-10,000 tons and measured 465-487 (w.1.). They mounted between one and four 5-inch guns and numerous 40mm. and 20mm. guns. Speed: 17-20 knots; aircraft: about 30.

Corvettes and Destroyer Escorts

WHEN THE BATTLE OF THE ATLANTIC BEGAN TO ASSUME MAJOR proportions, the British quickly realized that they did not have enough available destroyers to give adequate protection to the Atlantic convoys. In combating U-boats—especially U-boats attacking in wolf-packs— large numbers of escort vessels were essential. Some escorts had to be free to investigate distant contacts while the rest remained close to the vulnerable merchantmen.

At first the Royal Navy augmented its surface escort forces with sloops, a type roughly equivalent to American Coastguard cutters. Later, a specially designed anti-submarine type, the corvette, began to join the fleet in great numbers. Smaller, slower, more lightly armed and armored, the corvettes lacked the versatility of destroyers. They had only one intended function, to kill submarines, and this, with their load of detection and destruction devices, their great maneuverability and their specialist crews, they did admirably.

Corvettes have been credited with turning the tide of the Battle of the Atlantic. This claim may be arguable but what must certainly be granted is that British arms of all sorts played the major role in breaking the U-boat threat. Of the grand total of 768 German submarines sunk during the war, British forces accounted for 561.

The American equivalent of the corvette was the destroyer escort (DE). Somewhat superior to the corvettes, and produced in vast quantities, DE's served with both the Royal and U. S. Navies. With escort

U.S.S. **Durck** (D.E. 666) was typical of the great fleet of destroyer escorts which the U. S. Navy built during the war.

The Corvettes of the Flower class were the most numerous in the Royal Navy. They displaced about 925 tons and usually carried a 4-inch gun mounted forward of the bridge.

Patrol aircraft such as this U. S. Navy PBY Catalina and K-type blimp, played a major role in ASW operations in the Atlantic.

carriers and destroyers, they formed the basic elements of the hunter-killer teams which scoured the Atlantic after 1943.

Curiously enough, the most famous incident involving a DE occurred not in the Atlantic but in the Pacific, where enemy submarine activity was never a major factor.

In the spring of 1944, the Japanese, realizing that the Americans were planning a major offensive somewhere in the Western Pacific, assembled a large battle fleet in the Philippines. In order to protect against a possible American thrust south of Truk, Admiral Toyoda set up a scouting line of six submarines across the approaches to Palau. On May 17, the DE *England* found and sank one of these scouts. On May 22, *England* found and sank another. Fantastically, in the next eight days, *England* sank all the rest, a feat unequalled in naval history.

Toyoda did not know what had obliterated his scouting line but he assumed that it could have been nothing less than an entire American fleet. Accordingly he shifted his defenses south to the Pelews. He was thus totally unprepared for the true site of the American attack: Saipan.

TECHNICAL NOTES: The U. S. DE's averaged 1,140-1,450 tons displacement and measured 289-306 ft. (o.a.). Armament varied from three 3-inch and four 40mm. guns to two 5-inch and ten 40mm. guns. Speed: 19-24 knots. Flower class corvettes displaced 925 tons, were armed with one 4-inch and several smaller guns and had a speed of 17 knots. Both types carried large quantities of ASW gear.

U.S. and British Submarines

THE BATTLE OF THE ATLANTIC WAS A DUEL BETWEEN THE U-BOATS AND developing Allied ASW techniques. In the Pacific, the Japanese lacked both the techniques and the necessary command of the surface of the sea to make their anti-submarine operations effective. The price they paid for this failure was staggering.

America's undersea offensive against Japan was brilliantly conceived and conducted. Japan's supply lines were methodically cut and her merchant shipping was nearly exterminated. Even though U. S. submarines sank less total tonnage than the U-boats, the ultimate effect of these sinkings was very nearly decisive. U. S. boats accounted for about 1,150 Japanese merchant ships—over half the available total—and 29 per cent of the total of naval vessels sunk. And still more were sunk by naval mines laid by submarines. Against this was balanced the loss of a total of 52 U. S. boats during the war.

The individual exploits of U. S. submarines were among the most astonishing and dramatic of the war. The submarine *Sailfish*, for example, engaged and sank the aircraft carrier *Chuyo* in the midst of a typhoon. *Archerfish*, close to the Japanese coast, sank the supercarrier *Shinano* just ten days after it had been launched (it was the largest warship ever sunk by a submarine). *Harder* probably sank a total of seven destroyers before she was herself sunk. Once, when caught on the surface by a destroyer, *Harder* calmly stood fast and fired three torpedoes to sink the charging enemy ship at point-blank range.

The American submarine **Archerfish** made the biggest kill in the history of undersea warfare when she sank the Japanese super-carrier **Shinano** (59,000 tons displacement) on November 29, 1944. **Shinano** had been in commission just ten days when **Archerfish** sent her to the bottom.

U.S.S. **Harder,** one of the most famous submarines of the war.

Boats of the **Sealion** type composed one of the Royal Navy's best-known submarine classes. One of them, **Seraph,** figured in the rescue of Gen. Giraud from France.

Typical of the fantastic exploits of U. S. submarines was the experience of *Tang* in the Formosa Straits in late 1944. On the night of October 24th, *Tang* surfaced in the middle of a heavily escorted Japanese convoy, reduced the convoy to a torpedo-battered shambles in a matter of minutes and escaped into the darkness, still running on the surface. The next night *Tang* repeated the same daring maneuver with another convoy. This time she was hit and sunk (ironically, by one of her own torpedoes), but not before she had sent her eighth merchantman in 24 hours to the bottom. Commander O'Kane, her skipper, won the Medal of Honor for his part in the action.

British submarines accounted for less total tonnage sunk than their American or German counterparts, but they gave place to none in aggressiveness and their effect on Axis shipping in the Mediterranean was relatively great.

Upholder, perhaps the most famous of the British submarines in the Mediterranean, operated out of Malta. Her record of 97,000 tons of enemy shipping sunk was the highest in the Royal Navy and was bettered by only two U. S. submarines. *Turbulent* made a reputation as one of the most audacious of British submarines. On one occasion she surfaced off the coast of Libya and, ignoring the danger from shore-based artillery, proceeded to shell one of Rommel's motor parks with her small deck gun. At another time she pressed home an attack on a small Italian convoy so vigorously that she sank every ship in it. *Seraph,* on the other hand, is best remembered for her part in secret missions such as the rescue of General Giraud from France and the delivery of General Mark Clark to North Africa prior to Operation Torch.

TECHNICAL NOTES: U. S. Fleet submarines displaced 1,525 tons and measured 311.8 ft. (o.a.). Armament included one or two 5-inch, one 40 mm. and one 20mm. gun plus ten 21-inch torpedo tubes. Speed: 10 knots submerged; 20 knots, surface. British Trident class submarines displaced 1,575 tons, had ten 21-inch torpedo tubes and a speed of 15 knots, surface.

Landing Craft

DURING THE YEARS BEFORE WORLD WAR II THE TIME-HONORED MILITARY device of invasion by sea came, in some quarters, to be regarded with increasing suspicion. It began to seem doubtful, thanks to modern technology, that successful beachheads could be established in the face of strong enemy opposition. The range of coastal artillery and the effectiveness of land-based bombers were formidable enough obstacles, but even more difficult was the logistic problem. Modern armies require vast quantities of heavy equipment, fuel and supplies. How, in the absence of docking facilities, could these be successfully conveyed to the troops on the beach?

The answer—and it was an answer which was vital to the prosecution of the Allies' offensive strategy—lay in the creation of what amounted to a whole new complex of military operations: amphibious warfare. And the technological innovation which made amphibious warfare possible was the development of a fleet of shallow-draught vessels capable of disgorging battle-ready men and heavy cargoes directly on the contested beaches themselves, hundreds of miles from the staging areas.

The first Allied war-time experiments in the use of landing craft were made by the British. Between June, 1940 and March, 1942 a series of daring Commando raids on enemy-held positions in Norway and France demonstrated the effectiveness of small landing craft in putting troops ashore for limited objectives. In August, 1942, at Dieppe, a more

British troops pour ashore on the Isle of Elba from U. S.-built LCI's (Landing Craft Infantry).

American LSMR's (converted LSM's) launch a barrage of 4.5-inch rockets at the Japanese island of Tokishiki Shima.

The backbone of the American amphibious forces was the big tank-carrying LST.

impressive amphibious demonstration was made. 10,000 men in 200 ships—some of them (American LCT's) carrying 40-ton Churchill tanks—went ashore in the face of savage German resistance and accomplished most of the things they had set out to do.

But it remained for the Americans to convert amphibious warfare from a tactic to a strategy. Indeed, the nature of the Pacific war left the United States no choice. From American shipyards came an armada of queer-looking vessels, ranging in size from the great 457-foot Landing Ship Dock (LSD) to 25-foot amphibious tracked vehicles (LVT). There were 327-foot Landing Ship Tank's (LST); 200-foot all purpose Landing Ship Medium's (LSM); 158-foot Landing Craft Infantry's (LCI); 50-foot Landing Craft Medium's (LCM); and many more. From Guadalcanal on they participated in every island assault in the Pacific, every sea-borne invasion in the Mediterranean, and the great climax of amphibious operations, Operation Overlord.

Although not primarily lethal weapons in the same sense as, say, fighter planes or submachine guns, landing craft of all sorts were often directly involved in combat. Most carried some sort of offensive armament and the larger types mounted a fairly impressive collection of anti-aircraft and even 5-inch weapons. Some LCI's were especially armed and employed as escort gunboats. The little 25-foot LVT's were, in effect, pure assault weapons, being amphibious tracked vehicles which ran up onto the beach along with the troops and assumed the functions of light tanks. Finally, the LCI's and LSM's, their well decks crammed with 4.5-inch rocket launchers, became some of the most awe-inspiring shore bombardment vessels ever to see action.

TECHNICAL NOTES: U. S. LST's had a beaching displacement of 2,366 tons, a troop capacity of 175 and a speed of 11.6 knots. In addition to transporting tanks and other vehicles, oceangoing LST's could also transport smaller landing craft such as LCT's.

Miniature Submarines

IN RETROSPECT, THE USE OF MINIATURE SUBMARINES IN WORLD WAR II seems bizarre, yet like some other strange weapons, the tiny craft managed to do a certain amount of rather important damage. Britain, Italy, Germany and Japan built and employed various forms of the undersea weapon.

The British called their miniature submarines "X-craft," and built a flotilla of them for the express purpose of attacking and destroying the great ships of the German Navy—*Tirpitz, Scharnhorst,* and *Lutzow*—which raided Allied supply convoys in the North Sea from carefully guarded anchorages in the fjords of Norway. In September, 1943, three X-craft found *Tirpitz* at her berth in Altenfjord. Although one of the midgets became fouled in the nets surrounding the giant battleship and was lost and the remaining two were detected almost immediately, one, the X-7, succeeded in laying charges under *Tirpitz*. The midget was lost and her crew taken prisoner, but the explosive blow dealt *Tirpitz* was enough to put her out of commission for months and leave her permanently crippled. British Lancaster bombers later completed the job begun by the X-craft.

The British midgets also struck at the Japanese. On the night of July 30, 1945, two X-craft entered Singapore harbor and frogmen from XE-3 attached limpet mines to the hull of the IJN cruiser *Tokao* (which had been damaged by torpedoes from U. S. S. *Darter* on the eve of the Battle of Leyte Gulf and had returned to Singapore for repairs). *Tokao*

The British "X" class miniature submarines were 48-ft. long and carried a crew of four. They carried no torpedoes, only limpet mines which had to be attached to the hull of their targets by frogmen. The later improved "XE" boats carried a 5-man crew.

168

This Japanese miniature submarine was captured by U. S. forces in Hawaii the day after Pearl Harbor. It had been transported across the Pacific by an "I" class ocean-going submarine, for it had, itself, only a 200-mile cruising radius.

The top half of a German "Negro" manned torpedo. This was the carrier vehicle; beneath was attached a normally-loaded electric torpedo.

was virtually blown out of the water; both midgets made good their escape.

In their area of operation, the Mediterranean, Italian miniature submarines (actually, manned torpedoes) achieved the same sort of success as the British X-craft. On December 19, 1941, an Italian midget penetrated the defenses of Alexandria Harbor. Its crew successfully attached limpet mines to the Royal Navy battleships *Queen Elizabeth* and *Valiant*, riding at anchor in the Egyptian port, and damaged both badly.

Japanese miniature submarines were extensively used, but with virtually no success. They first went into action on December 7, 1941, at Pearl Harbor, where they accomplished nothing. This initial lack of success became standard. During the entire war, Japanese midgets sank only one ship—not a major combatant—and lightly damaged another. In the end, they were largely relegated to ferrying supplies.

Germany, as might be expected, experimented extensively with both miniature submarines and manned torpedoes. Called "Beavers" and "Seals" by the Germans, the two main types of miniature submarines sank a couple of transports in the Channel in the months after D-day and accounted for nearly 90,000 tons of light shipping in the Scheldt Estuary between December, 1944, and April, 1945.

The German manned torpedoes were not very successful, but were technically interesting. In the "Negro," the most prominent type, the pilot rode in a manually-controlled electric torpedo whose warhead had been removed. The pilot's head was encased in a 20-inch plexiglass dome which barely protruded from the water. Attached beneath this odd vehicle rode a normally loaded electric torpedo which could be launched at the pilot's command. Benefiting from surprise, one of these contraptions managed to score a hit on a British light cruiser in the Orne Estuary, but once Allied gunners were alerted to the danger, the manned torpedoes became sitting ducks. No more successful attacks were made and combat losses rose to nearly 80 per cent. The U. S. destroyer *Madison* sank five such craft in the Mediterranean in a single day.

TECHNICAL NOTES: The Japanese midget submarines usually measured about 79 ft. (o.a.), had a maximum surface speed of 24 knots, and carried two 18-inch torpedoes. The "X" craft measured 48 ft. (o.a.) and were armed with limpet mines. Both types of craft were transported over long distances by regular oceangoing submarines. The Italian manned torpedoes were about 22 ft. long, carried one or two men in dorsal seats and had a detachable warhead which could be fixed to the hull of the target vessel manually.

Torpedo Boats

DURING THE 1890's, AT THE HEIGHT OF THE ANGLO-FRENCH NAVAL
rivalry, the white hope of the French Navy's "jeune ecole" was a formidable new weapon: the motor torpedo boat. Armed with the then-novel Whitehead torpedo, the French MTB's were intended to attack every existing class of British ship and, by virtue of their great speed and maneuverability, remain relatively impervious to the menace of British naval ordnance. It was in order to meet the threat of the MTB's that the British constructed the world's first modern destroyers.

At the beginning of World War II, MTB's were no longer considered major naval weapons. Britain's R. N. Coastal Patrol boasted only 40 officers and 200 ratings in 1939, and the United States entered the war with only twelve PT boats in service.

But the torpedo boats quickly proved their value in combat. By 1943 the British Coastal Patrol had swollen to 2,000 officers and 15,000 ratings, and MTB actions in the Channel and North Sea were averaging one per night. The Royal Navy's renewed emphasis on MTB's was largely accounted for by the increasing activity of their German counterparts in attacking Channel convoys. Volumes could be written about the hundreds of gallant, deadly battles fought between the British MTB's and MGB's (motor gun boats) and the so-called German E-boats (a catch-all classification covering about six types). The end result of this war of attrition, combined with the blows dealt by Allied air power, was that Germany had only a little more than 30 torpedo boats with

A British Vospar-type MTB makes a high-speed foray into the English Channel. The MTB was the British equivalent of the American PT boat.

An American PT Boat (PT 117) showing one of the standard arrangements of external equipment.

The generic name for all German torpedo boats was "E-boats." The diesel-powered craft in this picture properly belonged to the "S" class.

which to resist the great Allied invasion fleet which crossed the Channel on June 6, 1944.

The American PT boat forces underwent a similar, even greater, expansion after the beginning of hostilities. Blooded early, the six PT's based in the Philippines made an international reputation for themselves in the months following Pearl Harbor. At the Battle of Midway, ten PT's were available to supplement the American surface fleet. For nine months, between the invasion of North Africa and the invasion of Sicily, a squadron of PT's was the sole permanent representative of the U. S. Navy in the Mediterranean. In growing numbers, PT's participated in every major Solomons naval engagement after October, 1942. By October, 1944, so many PT's were available that Admiral Kinkaid was able to throw, on short notice, an advance force of forty-five boats against the Nishimura battle fleet which entered Surigao Strait on the fateful night of the 24th.

MTB's and PT's, despite the undeniable value of their services, were operationally limited. Essentially short-range, calm-water craft, they could not operate effectively across long distances at sea or in the kind of bad weather conditions which prevailed in the Aleutians. Hence their association with operations in the Channel, the Mediterranean and among the island chains in the Pacific.

American and British torpedo boats were mostly Vospar-, Electric Boat-, or Higgins-built craft, constructed of plywood and mounting two or four torpedo tubes. Deck armament usually included 20mm. Oerlikon cannon and machine guns, and occasionally a 40mm. Bofors. Many of the boats were capable of speeds well in excess of 40 knots. The best German boats, the "S" class vessels, were larger and slower than the Anglo-American craft, and carried mines in addition to torpedoes.

TECHNICAL NOTES: U. S. Torpedo Boats built by Higgins and Electric Boat displaced 35 tons, measured 81 ft. (o.a.), and were powered by three Packard V-12 engines. Top speed was 40 to 45 knots. Armament included two 21- or four 18-inch torpedo tubes, two 20mm. or 25mm. AA guns, and eight depth charges. Standard British Torpedo Boats displaced 28-32 tons, measured about 72 ft. (o.a.), had a top speed of about 44 knots. Armament usually included two 21-inch torpedo tubes and two 20mm. Oerlikon cannon.

TANKS AND TANK DESTROYERS

TANKS WERE NEITHER NEW NOR UNTRIED WHEN WORLD WAR II BEGAN.
They had demonstrated at Cambrai in 1917 how devastatingly effective
they could be. But the importance of tanks in World War II was so
enormous as to overshadow all their previous history and to exceed the
anticipations of all but their most ardent interbellum proponents.

There was, in 1939, no consensus as to what kind of tank would
ultimately prove to be most effective. As the war progressed, however,
heavily armed mediums emerged as the best all-round fighters. Until the
end of the war the heavies tended to be too unwieldy and the light tanks,
under-armored. But the best mediums, such as the German Panther and
the Soviet T-34, managed to combine speed, fire power and protection
in a thoroughly formidable amalgam.

One war-time development about which opinions still differ was the
so-called "tank destroyer." This was essentially a powerful anti-tank gun
mounted on a regular (usually lightly-armored) tank chassis. The United
States, dissatisfied with its standard M4 medium tanks, looked on its
TD's as a quick, relatively inexpensive way of increasing the offensive
quality of its armored forces. The Germans and the Russians, on the
other hand, were content with their medium and heavy tanks but used
TD's to augment the *size* of their armored forces. The often clumsy
and vulnerable TD's were never a match for comparably armed tanks,
but they had their value, *faute de mieux.*

In a war where, as many said, "armor was king," the German tanks
and tank destroyers were generally the best. Perhaps more than the
aircraft of the *Luftwaffe* or the U-boats of the *Kriegsmarine,* tanks sym-
bolize the rise and fall of German arms in World War II. They were the
spearhead of the panzer units which made *Blitzkrieg* a household word
in the early forties. And, in the end, they were the grisly rearguard in
the desperate, hopeless struggle to avert the annihilation of Hitler's
"1000-year Reich."

The U. S. M5 Light Tank

BEFORE THE WAR IT USED TO BE FASHIONABLE TO REFER TO THE
armored forces as "the iron cavalry." However much the phrase betrayed
a misunderstanding of the role of tanks in general, it applied well enough
to the light tanks. For these fast, lightly armed and armored vehicles
played much the same role as the chasseurs and hussars of the Napo-
leonic era.

They were excellent for executing small, rapid flanking movements,
for punching holes in enemy lines, for suppressing machine gun fire, for
cutting through forward lines of communication. Conversely, they were
not supposed to be capable of lending significant artillery support or of
engaging in battles with heavier enemy tanks.

Light tanks performed everywhere and well in the early war years.
Nine-ton German PzKw II's ran wild through the disorganized infantries
of Poland, the Netherlands, and France; British Bren carriers, Cruisers
and Stuarts fared splendidly against the lightly armed Italians in North
Africa; and little Soviet T-40's and T-70's did useful work for Russia
after the turn of the tide at Moscow.

But the trend was toward heavier equipment: medium and heavy
tanks, big tank-destroyers, and large calibre anti-tank guns like the German high velocity 75mm. and "88." The importance of the "little
fellows" dwindled. Of the many light tanks in service at the beginning
of hostilities, only a few continued to play important roles through to
the end of the war.

The M5A1 was the standard U. S. light tank throughout most of
the war. It was introduced in 1942 in time to take part in the
landings near Casablanca.

These German PzKw I light tanks were rolling into Poland when this photograph was taken. Soon after the war began, the PzKw I was entirely replaced by the larger PzKw II.

Armed solely with Vickers .303 machine guns, the British Mk. VI A light tank performed well in the early western desert campaigns but was later outclassed by the armor and AT weapons of the Africa Korps.

Of these, the most outstanding was undoubtedly the American M5 series. The reason for the M5's longevity lay not only in its qualitative excellence but in the fact that, until the end of the war, the U. S. lacked sufficient Sherman medium tanks to meet its far-flung commitments. M5's were available, they could be transported across oceans easily and they could be put onto enemy beaches from relatively small landing craft.

Thus M5's went ashore with Patton in North Africa; accompanied the first assault units in Sicily, Italy and Southern France; and stormed into Normandy with the D day forces. Even more important, they provided the armored backbone for almost all of the island invasions in the Pacific and proved themselves first-rate jungle fighters.

The standard M5A1 was a 16.9-ton, 36 m.p.h. machine, mounting a small 37mm. cannon in a prism-shaped turret and carrying a secondary armament of two .30 cal. machine guns. It had an automatic hydraulic transmission system which eliminated gear shifting.

Although the M5 was theoretically incapable of doing battle with heavier tanks, it sometimes had to. Once in Sicily a group of M5's contrived to knock out fifteen German PzKw IV's—25-tonners mounting 75mm. cannon—and lost only three of their own.

In 1943, in response to the demand for more powerful armor, the U. S. produced a formidable new light tank called the M24. Nearly as fast as the M5 and only three tons heavier, the M24 carried a two-inch mortar and a 75mm. gun in its slab-sided turret. The M24 saw considerable combat in Europe and the island campaigns, and, in post-war years it replaced the veteran M5A1.

TECHNICAL NOTES: The M5A1 Light Tank had a combat weight of 16.9 tons, a top speed of 36 m.p.h., two 130 h.p. Cadillac V-8 cylinder engines, a hydramatic transmission, vertical volute spring suspension, 1.5-inch front and turret armor, one 37mm. gun M6, two .30 cal. machine guns, and a four-man crew.

The U.S. M4 Medium Tank

THE HULKING M4—DUBBED THE "GENERAL SHERMAN" BY THE BRITISH —was America's standard medium tank throughout most of the war. And since the United States possessed no heavy tank, the Sherman was obliged to perform the functions of a "heavy" as well. It was sometimes inadequate to the tasks assigned it—lacking the brilliance of the Panther and the T-34 or the rugged power of the Tiger and the Stalin. But the Sherman was solid, reliable and exceptionally versatile. Great numbers of the tank, sagaciously employed, earned the Sherman its reputation as a capital weapon in North Africa, Italy, France and Germany.

The Sherman was a hasty replacement for the M3 "General Grant" with which the United States entered the war. The Grant had been, by any standards, unimpressive. Its 75mm. main armament had been mounted in the hull rather than in a turret and consequently could traverse only a few degrees independently. Dangerously high in silhouette, many Grants were of riveted construction. When the riveted Grant was hit by an enemy AT shell, these rivets would explode, flying about the tank's interior like shrapnel.

The Sherman was founded on the Grant's chassis but otherwise was a completely new tank. Its silhouette was lowered, its hull was either welded or cast and its 75mm. gun was mounted in a fully-rotating turret.

According to one British tank expert, "There is little doubt that the Sherman was one, probably the main, deciding factor in our victory (in North Africa)." About 400 Shermans had been rush-delivered to

Shermans move up an Italian hillside. The tank in the foreground is a welded-hull M-4A4; third in line is a cast-hull M-4A1. All mount 75mm. M3 guns.

An M-4A3E8 Sherman mounting a 76mm. gun. This tank also featured an improved horizontal suspension system.

An American M-3 medium tank with riveted hull. Some other versions had cast or welded hulls.

the British Eighth Army before it fell back to its last-ditch position at El Alamein. In company with British Crusaders and Valentines, following a devastating five-hour British artillery assault on the German minefields and fortifications, the Shermans were hurled into the 12-day battle which turned the tide of victory against Rommel. The Afrika Korps' PzKw III's and IV's, which previously held the edge in the desert, were overwhelmed. More than 200 of them were knocked out in a single day of fighting.

From then on, both in Europe and the Pacific, ever-increasing numbers of Shermans were in the vanguard of the relentless Anglo-American drive to victory on land. Hundreds of Shermans poured onto the D-day beaches in Normandy, protected by special sealing and canvas-rubber walls stretched round their hulls (these were DD [Duplex Drive] Shermans which propelled themselves in water or on land).

The versatility of the Sherman is exemplified by the variations which took place in its armament during the later stages of the war. In a toughened, redesigned turret the U. S. Army placed a more powerful 76mm. gun and the British, a similar 17-lb. gun. Other Sherman variants carried a 105mm. howitzer in their turrets and still others mounted 60-tube racks of 4.5-inch rocket launchers. The M4 chassis was also the basis for most of the major U. S. self-propelled guns and tank destroyers.

The Sherman was patently not the best medium tank of the war but it performed well in all of the roles appropriate to its characteristics. And in the hands of brilliant generals such as Montgomery or Patton, Shermans could not only be formidable but, often, decisive.

TECHNICAL NOTES: A widely-used variant of the Sherman Medium Tank was the M4A4 having a combat weight of 36.25 tons, a top speed of 25 m.p.h., a 430 h.p. Chrysler six cylinder engine, synchromesh transmission, horizontal spring suspension, 2-inch front and 3.2-inch turret armor, one 75mm. gun M3, two .30 cal. machine guns, and a five-man crew.

U. S. Tank Destroyers

THE CONTINUING DIFFICULTIES WHICH ALLIED TANKS EXPERIENCED IN dealing with Germany's powerful armored forces gave rise, inevitably, to the creation of that class of weapons known as tank destroyers. The tank destroyers were essentially powerful higher-velocity guns mounted on standard tank chassis. They could inflict much greater damage than could the normal 75mm. and 6-lb. guns carried by the Sherman and Churchill tanks, but a reduction in armor to give them more speed made them particularly vulnerable. They were not a wholly satisfactory substitute for powerful heavy tanks, but they did manage to perform very effectively in certain situations.

The first important American TD was known as the M10 Gun Motor Carriage. It was used effectively in North Africa and pointed the way towards more sophisticated designs.

The M10 was a true tank destroyer, not a self-propelled assault gun used in a dual role. It mounted a 3-inch high-velocity gun in a shallow open turret set on a Sherman chassis. It was relatively fast and maneuverable and performed well when it was first introduced during the closing days of the North African campaign. In one 25-minute skirmish near Bizerte, a single M10 destroyed four German tanks, an 88mm. gun and a number of small combat vehicles including an armored car.

In Europe, M10's shared honors with still more advanced TD's. The M18 used a 76mm. gun mounted in an open turret placed on the chassis of the new M24 light tank. The M18 was lightly armored and

The M-10, mounting a 3-inch gun in an open-topped turret, was America's first true tank destroyer. This M-10, on a dug-in ramp in a German field, is being used as a stationary artillery piece.

The M-18 Hellcat carried a 76mm. M1A1 gun on a light tank chassis.

The M-36 was the only armored vehicle to carry a 90mm. gun into action for the Allies in World War II.

therefore vulnerable to enemy AT fire, but it did have an impressive top speed of 45 m.p.h. The M36, on the other hand, was essentially an M10 with a redesigned turret and a modified 90mm. anti-aircraft gun. It represented a late-war effort to improve the major weapon on American tanks. This big gun subsequently equipped the 46-ton M26 "General Pershing" medium tank introduced in the last six weeks of the war in Europe.

The American TD's sustained fairly high losses, and towards the end of the war the Germans developed tactics and weapons which greatly reduced their effectiveness. But the TD's nevertheless inflicted severe damage on the enemy. Patton's Third Army, for example, claimed that in 231 days of campaigning in France and Germany its TD's had knocked out 648 German tanks, 211 SP guns, 349 AT guns, 175 artillery pieces, 801 bunkers and pill boxes and 1,556 miscellaneous vehicles. Even though these figures may be subject to adjustment, they suggest that the TD's did in fact play an important role.

TECHNICAL NOTES: The tank destroying M18 Gun Motor Carriage had a combat weight of 19.5 tons, a top speed of 45 m.p.h., a 400 h.p. Continental nine cylinder radial engine, torsion bar suspension, .5-inch front and side and .75-inch turret front armor, one 76mm. gun M1A1, one .50 cal. machine gun, and a five-man crew. The tank destroying M36 Gun Motor Carriage had a combat weight of 30.5 tons, a top speed of 26 m.p.h., a 450 h.p. Ford V-8 cylinder engine, vertical volute spring suspension, 1.5-inch front and .75-inch turret armor, one 90mm. gun M3, and one .50 cal. machine gun.

The German PzKw IV Medium Tank

TANK WARFARE WAS AN INTEGRAL PART OF GERMANY'S MILITARY PLANS almost from the moment Hitler came to power. British and French tanks had contributed largely to the defeat of the Kaiser's armies in World War I. Mindful of this, the Nazis were resolved that what happened then would not be duplicated. Therefore, coincident with the creation and development of the *Luftwaffe*—and as much in secret—a thoroughly equipped and trained tank force was built.

Foremost among the German tanks encountered by the Allies during the opening half of World War II were the PzKw III and its combat companion the PzKw IV. Both were medium cruiser tanks, highly maneuverable, well-armed, and armored. They were used in overrunning Poland and the Low Countries and saw abundant action against the British and French in the fighting that ended with Dunkirk and the fall of France.

The PzKw IV was the better tank. It was heavier than its 18-ton stablemate, and possessed a larger gun. From its introduction in 1937, until American M3 and M4 medium tanks fought against it in North Africa, the tank carried a short 75mm. howitzer. The gun was mounted in a shallow, closed turret set almost dead-center on the tank's low, wide chassis. In this form, PzKw IV's backed up the hordes of PzKw III's that composed the heart of the armored force that opened Germany's attack and invasion of Russia in 1941.

In 1942, however, commensurate with the increased armor of Brit-

This PzKw IV medium tank mounting a long 75mm. gun was knocked out of action in·North Africa.

A PzKw IV with a short 75mm. gun rolls into a small town in the Polish Corridor.

A PzKw III with a long 50mm. gun. Other versions carried short 75mm. guns or flamethrowers.

ish tanks and the battle debut of the American Sherman, the short howitzer was exchanged for a long-barreled 75mm. higher velocity gun. The PzKw IV also was equipped with more and thicker armor and fitted with wire mesh screens or steel plates on the sides of the hull to protect it against the Sunday punch of the American anti-tank rocket-firing bazooka.

Following the defeat of France and the shift of major land operations to North Africa, both the PzKw III and IV appeared on the Libyan and Egyptian deserts. The British and French were administering a blistering defeat to the Italians, and Rome looked to Berlin to pull the fat out of the fire. German aid took the form of the Afrika Korps. A nucleus of what was to become one of the most famous fighting units in the war arrived on the North African front early in 1941.

On March 30, 1941, an armada of PzKw IIIs, IVs, armored cars, 88mm. anti-tank guns, and motorized infantry—supported by *Stuka* dive bombers—began Germany's first desert battle with the British. It drove them from El Agheila, past Tobruk, to Salum. The German tanks demonstrated an overwhelming superiority. At the Battle of Salum, more than 100 British tanks, including heavy Matilda II's, light Mark VI's, and new, speedy Mark II medium cruisers, were outgunned and destroyed. Only a dozen PzKw III's and IV's were lost, and few of them to hits scored by British tanks.

The PzKw IV continued in service to the end of the war, although its pre-eminence in the Panzer units was gradually usurped by Panther and Tiger tanks. Its chassis, however, was most effectively used as the basis for several of the larger German self-propelled guns.

TECHNICAL NOTES: In its most advanced variant the PzKw IV Medium Tank had a combat weight of 27.6 tons, a top speed of 25 m.p.h., a 300 h.p. Maybach V-12 cylinder engine, synchromesh transmission, elliptic spring suspension, 3.4-inch front and 2-inch turret armor, one 75mm. gun KwK 40, two 7.9mm. machine guns, and a five-man crew.

The German Panther Tank

WHEN GERMANY INVADED RUSSIA IN JUNE, 1941, PZKW III AND IV TANKS were, as usual, the backbone of the Panzer forces. The Germans knew that Russia possessed some good tanks but assumed that they would neither be available in sufficient quantities nor be used with skill. The headlong pace of the German assault on the central front, the disorganization of the Red Army, the vast encirclements—all seemed to bear out Hitler's predictions of an early victory and tended to obscure the threat implicit in occasional examples of Russia's ability to use modern armored equipment effectively.

But with the German failure to take Moscow, and the sudden, alarming development of a Russian counter-offensive in the winter of 1941, Germany's illusions began to disintegrate. One of the most unpleasant surprises for Germany was the emergence of large numbers of Soviet T-34 medium tanks. These fine mass-produced machines soon ran roughshod over the PzKw III's and IV's and threatened to cancel the armored supremacy on which Germany's *Blitzkrieg* tactics depended.

Germany's technological response to the menace of the T-34 was a new medium-heavy tank, the Panther. The Panther was vastly superior to the T-34. It was a superb machine, easily out-classing any comparable Western tanks. Its 49 tons could move across level terrain at over 30 m.p.h. Its long-barreled 75mm. gun had a large chamber which gave ultra-high velocity to its special armor-piercing shells. It used direct sights up to a distance of 1,640 yards and could punch holes in the heaviest

A German Panther tank knocked out by American guns in France. The Panther was probably the best all-round tank of the war. Note the anti-magnetic plaster spread on the tank's armor.

Rear view of a Panther wrecked during the invasion of Germany.

The Hunting Panther was an 88mm. (PAK 43) gun mounted on a Panther chassis. It was one of the most formidable German tank destroyers.

British or American tank armor. The Panther was highly maneuverable, carried 4.3-inch turret armor and could be modified to ford relatively deep streams.

Along with her variety of medium and heavy tanks, tank destroyers, and self-propelled guns, the Panther was the keystone of Germany's armored defense against the Anglo-American invasion of Europe and the great Russian offensives in the east. It performed with distinction against Shermans, Churchills and T-34's, and was overwhelmed rather than overmatched by its opponents.

As with most German tanks, the Panther's chassis was used as the basis for a tank destroyer. An 88mm. gun was fitted into a slightly built-up Panther hull and the resulting machine was named the Hunting Panther. Combining as it did Germany's best tank chassis and best anti-tank gun, the Hunting Panther was a lethal weapon indeed.

TECHNICAL NOTES: The Panther Heavy-medium Tank had a combat weight of 49 tons, a top speed of 30 m.p.h., a 700 h.p. Maybach V-12 cylinder engine, synchromesh transmission, torsion bar suspension, 3.2-inch front and 4.3-inch turret armor, one 75mm. gun KwK 42, two 7.9mm. machine guns, and a five-man crew.

The German Tiger Tank

ONE OF THE MOST AWESOME TANKS TO PARTICIPATE IN THE WAR WAS the massive German Tiger. When the first 60-ton versions of the monster appeared in the final phases of the North African campaign, British and American gunners were shocked to see their 6-lb. and 75mm. shells literally bounce off the Tiger's armor plate. Only by knocking off its treads could the huge tank be stopped.

The Tiger had been intended primarily for use on the Russian front and although it was successful there, its low speed and lack of maneuverability somewhat vitiated its effectiveness on the broad Russian plains. In Italy, too, the Tigers were seriously hampered by the roughness of the terrain and the lack of roads and bridges on which they could safely navigate.

In Western Europe, however, operational conditions for the Tiger were good, and the tank became one of the most formidable opponents of the British and American forces driving eastward from the Normandy beachheads, although it did not appear in great numbers. By this time the Tiger had been considerably improved from its original form. In its last and best version it was known as the Tiger II or King Tiger. Somewhat resembling a scaled-up Panther, the King Tiger weighed close to 80 tons. It was armed with a high-velocity super 88mm. gun and a variety of machine guns. Its enormous treads measured 32 inches across, its turret armor was over seven inches thick and its glacis plate was six inches thick. Over-all sealing and telescopic air intakes permitted the King Tiger to ford small rivers up to sixteen feet deep.

A 75-ton King Tiger tank rumbles into action on the western front. Heavily armed and armored, the King Tiger was nevertheless underpowered.

Early versions of the Tiger were also known as the PzKw VI. They weighed over 60 tons and mounted 88mm. KwK36 guns.

The Hunting Tiger, the tank destroyer version of the Tiger, mounted a 128mm. gun in its built-up hull.

The tank's main defect still lay in its clumsiness and relative lack of speed. A 700 h.p. 12-cylinder engine, the same used in the Panther, gave the King Tiger a scant 17 m.p.h. top speed and left it vulnerable to certain natural tank traps. Often the Germans simply dug Tigers into shallow pits and used them as stationary pill boxes.

Tiger chassis were also used to carry tank destroyer weapons. The most familiar of these, during the middle and late war years, was called "Ferdinand" by the Allies. "Ferdinand" was a 70-ton vehicle carrying an 88mm. gun housed in a large fully armored compartment atop the hull. Some of "Ferdinand's" armor was as much as eight inches thick but the machine was even slower than the Tiger and was vulnerable to attack from the sides and rear. An even larger self-propelled gun based on the Tiger chassis, the so-called Hunting Tiger, will be discussed later in connection with other German SP weapons.

TECHNICAL NOTES: The Tiger Heavy Tank had a combat weight of 62.8 tons, a top speed of 23 m.p.h., a 650 h.p. Maybach V-12 cylinder engine, torsion bar suspension, 4-inch front and turret armor, one 88mm. gun KwK 36, two 7.9mm. machine guns, and a five-man crew. The Tiger II or King Tiger Heavy Tank had a combat weight of 76.9 tons, a top speed of 17 m.p.h., a 700 h.p. Maybach V-12 cylinder engine, torsion bar suspension, 5.9-inch front and 7.3-inch turret armor, one 88mm. gun KwK 43, two 7.9mm. machine guns, and a five-man crew.

The British Churchill Tank

ALTHOUGH THE BRITISH WERE THE FIRST TO USE TANKS IN WAGING A war, and were therefore fully cognizant of their value both as offensive and defensive weapons, the tanks with which they began World War II were considerably inferior in the most important respect—gunpower—to the German armor used against them in France and throughout most of the long, bitter North African campaign. But Britain used the tanks she possessed with great courage and brilliance. Quantity, resourcefulness, and strategy made her heavy Matilda II, light Mark VI, Mark II, Crusader, and Valentine tanks effective weapons against the elite German Afrika Korps in the savage, far-ranging battles of men and armor in the desert between El Alamein and Tunis. And with the introduction of the heavily-armed 43-ton Churchill, she at last matched the enemy.

First made part of the Royal Armored Force in 1940, the Churchill was as efficient in its job as the man for whom it was named. Early models of the tank cut their battle teeth against German armor in 1942, during the gallant but ill-fated British raid on Dieppe. Later, Churchills appeared in North Africa in the savage tank battles around Tunis and Bizerte; and again in Italy. When the Allies landed in France and the gigantic combined force of American and British military might embarked upon its relentless thrust to victory, large numbers of Churchill and narrow-tracked Covenanter medium tanks ground onto the continent. They hammered eastward across France from Caen, and north into Belgium to rout the enemy out of the Low Countries. Churchills

Churchill tanks of the Royal Armored Corps' 34th Tank Brigade roll along a road in Germany.

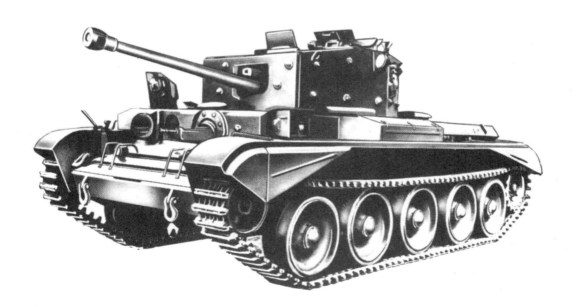

A British Crusader Mk. III medium tank goes over the top near Mersa Matruh. The Crusader carried a 6-lb. gun.

The British Matilda Mk. II heavy tank. Its armament consisted of a 2-lb. gun and a machine gun.

The Cromwell, a development of the Crusader, also carried a 6-lb. gun.

nobly acquitted themselves in the Battle of the Ardennes, swept into the Ruhr Valley, and pushed on to the Baltic Sea.

Heavily armored, and presenting a fairly low silhouette that made it a difficult target, the Churchill was powered by a 350 h.p. engine. It moved on full steel tracks at a top speed of 20 m.p.h. For a heavyweight, the tank was exceptionally maneuverable and moved with startling agility over any sort of terrain. It did combat with an assortment of armament, at different times mounting a 2-lb. gun, a 6-lb. gun, and a long-barreled 75mm. high-velocity gun, in a flat-topped turret set dead-center on the chassis. The Churchill also normally mounted two 7.92mm. Besa machine guns. Some models were equipped with a 76mm. howitzer in the front of the hull and some were used, terrifyingly, as giant flame throwers. A useful feature of the tank was its dual control system which permitted the front gunner to drive in the event the regular driver was unable to do so.

The Churchill, as well as the older Valentine and Matilda, were designated as infantry (i.e. heavy) tanks. British cruiser, or medium, tanks included the Covenanter, the Crusader, the Cavalier, the Cromwell, the Challenger, and the Comet. As the war progressed, cruiser tanks became increasingly heavy and powerful. Thus, confusingly, the last war-time cruiser, the Comet, was nearly twice as heavy and far better armed than the early-war Valentine infantry tank.

TECHNICAL NOTES: The Churchill Heavy Tank had a combat weight of 43.1 tons, a top speed of 20 m.p.h., a 350 h.p. Bedford Flat Twin Six (12 cylinder) engine, helical spring suspension, 3.46-inch front and turret armor, one 6-lb. gun MK V, two 7.9mm. Besa machine guns, and a five-man crew.

The Russian T-34 Tank

RUSSIAN TANKS, LIKE RUSSIAN AIRPLANES, WERE DEVELOPED SLOWLY and patiently over a long period. They were produced in enormous quantities, in keeping with the vast expanses they were created to defend. The Red Army was known to possess some 20,000 to 24,000 light, medium, and heavy tanks when Germany attacked the Soviet Union in the spring of 1941. Most, however, were obsolete and generally inferior to the armor of the invaders—a condition which contributed to the great German victories which opened the Russian campaign.

Some 17,000 Red tanks were destroyed in the first year of fighting on the Soviet's western front. But a prodigious production effort swiftly balanced the loss. By the end of 1942, new Russian tanks were grinding into battle in phenomenal quantities. Foremost among them, both in ability and number, was the T-34 medium tank, the "queen" of Russian armor and the root from which modern Soviet tank forces stemmed.

Redesigned many times after its origination in the early 1930s, the T-34 was put in mass production in 1939. It became the Red Army's standard medium tank in 1940 and served in that capacity through the Korean War, for which a number were supplied to the Chinese communists.

Every important feature of a great fighting tank was embodied in the T-34. It had speed, mobility, firepower, and good protective armor. A 500 h.p. diesel engine moved the tank at a top speed of more than 30 m.p.h., and consumed remarkably little fuel. The T-34 maneuvered

Soviet T-34's rumble through the streets of captured Leipzig. This original version of the T-34 carried a 76.2mm. M 1940 gun.

The improved T-34/85 was introduced in 1944. It carried an 85mm. M 1944 gun which could penetrate 4.7 inches of armor plate at 1,000 yards. This example was captured in Korea.

The T-70 was a Soviet light tank which mounted a 45mm. gun. The T-70 chassis was also used to carry a 76.2mm. SP gun.

quickly and easily on nearly two-foot wide tracks that took it through the worst mud and snow up to a yard deep.

For armament, the T-34 at first mounted a short 76.2mm. gun in its turret. This was later replaced by a long-barreled gun of the same calibre, and still later, at the war's end, by an 85mm. high-velocity gun. A 7.62mm. machine gun was set in the front of the hull, next to the driver.

Considered by some experts to be the finest tank to see action in World War II prior to the introduction of the Panther, the T-34 distinguished itself wherever it fought. In the Battle of Stalingrad, small groups of T-34's were deployed in a long series of harassing engagements with the enemy. They moved and struck fast, like hornets, with devastating effect. Their sting and stamina also yielded victorious results in the attacks and counterattacks which broke up the great German offensive against Kursk in July, 1943, and gave the Red Army the upper hand from then through the end of the war.

The Germans were quick to acclaim the combat ability of the T-34. They praised it as the best mid-war tank, and swiftly made it the model for their own excellent Panther medium tank. Indeed, the T-34 was everything the German experts judged it to be.

TECHNICAL NOTES: The T-34/85 Medium Tank, the most advanced of the T-34 design, had a combat weight of 34.4 tons, a top speed of 33 m.p.h., a 500 h.p. V-12 cylinder engine, Christie arm and coil spring suspension, 1.8-inch front and 3.7-inch turret armor, one 85mm. gun 1944, two 7.62mm. machine guns, and a four- to five-man crew.

The Russian JS Tank

THE RUSSIAN JS HEAVY TANK WAS DEVELOPED TO MEET THE CHALLENGE of Germany's formidable Panther, Tiger, and King Tiger tanks which had to some extent reestablished the superiority of Nazi armor following the widespread introduction of the Soviet T-34.

Commonly known as the Stalin, the JS was of a design developed from the KV series of heavy tanks and a furthering of the trend toward heavier and more powerfully armed equipment marked by the introduction of the KV-85.

Three versions of the Stalin heavy tank, the JS-I, II, and III, were produced in quantity. All three mounted the same main weapon—a high-velocity 122mm. gun, a giant step ahead in firepower from the 76.2mm. and 85mm. guns which equipped the KV-I, II, 85, and T-34/85 tanks.

JS-I's and II's first appeared in great numbers on the Soviet western front in the spring of 1944. The tanks played a leading role in the great Red Army offensive undertaken coincident with the British and American invasion of France. Stalins spearheaded the immense thrust of armor that balanced that of Patton and Montgomery, almost day for day, in closing the vise of defeat on Germany.

The first Stalin, the JS-I, weighed approximately 50 tons. Its high-velocity 122mm. gun was mounted in a large turret set well forward on a wide, squat chassis. Three 12.7mm D. Sh. K. machine guns completed its armament—one on top of the turret and two in the hull. The JS-II was similar, feature for feature, except that it had a much improved hull.

The Josef Stalin JS-1, mounting a 122mm. gun, was one of the war's finest heavy tanks. A later version, the JS-III is still one of the most formidable tanks in the world.

Russia's principal heavy tank prior to the advent of the Stalin was the KV. The KV-1C shown above weighed 52 tons and mounted a 76.2mm. gun.

The Stalin chassis was used to carry 122mm. and 152mm. SP artillery.

Stalin III's on parade.

The last and finest Stalin, the JS-III, introduced as the war ended, was a brilliant example of the high degree of tank development achieved by Russia after Germany attacked her. The country with the most, but the poorest tanks in 1941, Russia had the world's foremost armored force within two years.

The JS-III, in addition to its 122mm. gun, carried a 7.62mm. machine gun and sometimes a 12.7mm. machine gun on top of the turret for anti-aircraft defense.

In the Stalin, everything was pointed at function and performance. Crew space was exceedingly cramped in order to achieve the extremely low silhouette that made the tank a difficult target. The amount of ammunition carried for the tank's heavy gun was severely limited by a lack of storage space, and thus enforced the rule of making every shell count.

The armor of the Stalin was exceptional, both in strength and in arrangement. It was 4.85 inches thick on the JS-I and II, and 4.7 inches thick on the JS-III. Brought to a sloping point on the front of the latter, it gave the tank the appearance of a giant beetle. The angling of the armor in a three plane manner afforded the effect of greater thickness and made it almost impenetrable.

The forerunner of the Stalin, the KV, was also a prominent fighter. Mounting a 76.2mm. gun, it was the Red Army's basic heavy tank until the Stalin appeared.

When the Germans came up with their Tiger tank on the eastern front, the KV became the KV-85 by replacement of its 76.2mm. gun with an 85mm. intended to cope better with the 88mm. of the German tank.

Both Stalin and KV-85 tanks saw extensive combat during the final year of the war in Europe—in Poland, Czechoslovakia, Austria, and in Germany itself. The long range, powerful-hitting gun of the Stalin destroyed a fair share of the German armor knocked out as the Red Army converged on Berlin early in 1945.

TECHNICAL NOTES: The finest Stalin Heavy Tank, the JS-III, had a combat weight of 57 tons, a top speed of 20 m.p.h., a 600 h.p. V-12 cylinder engine, torsion bar suspension, 4.7-inch front armor, a turtle-back cast steel turret armored in varying thicknesses corresponding to the angle of penetration, one 122mm. gun 1944, one 7.62mm. machine gun and/or one 12.7mm. machine gun, and a five-man crew.

ARTILLERY

"IT IS WITH ARTILLERY," NAPOLEON ONCE REMARKED, "THAT WAR IS MADE."
Insofar as the observation was meant to pertain to the prevailing tactics
of the early nineteenth century, it was a very considerable exaggeration,
but by World War I it had come to seem almost prophetic. After Verdun,
artillery began to assume an importance hardly second to that of infantry
itself. Nor did this importance diminish in the Second World War.

Technically, most of the conventional artillery of World War II
was no more than a logical development of the ordnance of twenty years
before. The new weapons had, for their respective calibres, longer range,
better accuracy, greater velocity and so on; but, with few exceptions
(*e.g.,* automatic weapons such as the 40mm. Bofors) no new principles
were involved. A case in point is the famous German 88mm. gun which
was the direct descendant of a 1917 design.

In one important respect, however, many of the big guns of World
War II were far in advance of their predecessors. This was mobility. By
the war's end, the variety and quantity of self-propelled artillery in
service was bewildering, and even trailed weapons could be moved about
with great rapidity by specially designed prime movers. This mobility
was one of the major reasons why there was not in World War II the
kind of static trench warfare which characterized World War I.

More significant for the future were the new developments in un-
conventional artillery weapons: recoilless guns, rocket launchers and
ballistic missiles. These, coupled with nuclear explosives, pointed to a
time when the destructive potential of artillery would border on the
incalculable.

U. S. Self-Propelled Artillery

COMBINING THE MOBILITY OF THE TANK AND HALF-TRACK WITH THE long range, hard-hitting power of heavy artillery, self-propelled guns played a large part in the fighting on all fronts of World War II, for Allied and Axis forces alike. They were more easily and quickly put into action than trailered artillery, and could rapidly follow the course of battle. A majority of those used consisted of a heavy artillery piece mounted on a partially and lightly armored tank chassis. Designed for speed and maneuverability, the self-propelled gun, or gun motor carriage, could engage the enemy within a few minutes of halting, whereas it sometimes took up to an hour to emplace traditional vehicle-drawn artillery in order to fire.

A wide variety of full-tracked and half-tracked self-propelled guns were used by the Americans and British. One of the largest, brought into play following the Normandy invasion, was the U. S. M12 Gun Motor Carriage composed of a 155mm. gun on a modified M4 medium Sherman tank chassis. Extremely accurate, it hurled a 95-pound projectile over fifteen miles.

The 155mm. gun on the M12 was a World War I piece. The M40 mounted a more modern 155mm. M2 "Long Tom" gun also on a modified late Sherman chassis. This exceptionally powerful weapon was widely used in the ETO.

In supporting the fast, concentrated drive of Allied troops and tanks across France and through the Low Countries, great batteries of M12's

An M-12 Motor Gun Carriage prepares to fire on enemy targets in France. The M-12 used an M-4 tank chassis to mobilize a 155mm. M1917A1 gun of World War I vintage.

The British called the U. S. M-7 the "Priest." Mounting a 105mm. howitzer on a medium tank chassis, the M-7 was introduced to combat at the Battle of El Alamein.

The M-8 carried a 75mm. howitzer in a revolving turret set on a light tank chassis.

The M-40 was the 155mm. M2 "Long Tom" gun mounted on a medium tank chassis. Great numbers were used in the ETO.

were used to soften enemy fortifications prior to infantry and armor advances. They were particularly effective as part of the mammoth concentrations of artillery brought to bear upon German defenses on the borders of Belgium, Luxemburg, and France, and the Rhine River, in the fall, winter, and spring of 1944–45.

Another highly efficient Allied self-propelled gun was the famous M7, used extensively in North Africa, Sicily, and Italy, as well as in the Rhine Valley. Consisting of a 105mm. howitzer on a Sherman chassis, the M7 began its fighting career with the British Eighth Army at El Alamein in October, 1942. The British nicknamed the M7 "The Priest," because of a high pulpit-like round turret mounting a .50 cal. anti-aircraft machine gun at right front of the hull. They later produced their own version of the gun, called "The Bishop." It consisted of a 25-lb. gun mounted in a high box of armor on a Valentine tank chassis.

Priests and Bishops were used in Sicily and Italy, where their reliable performance on irregular terrain made them indispensable in tortuous mountain fighting.

The American M8 gun motor carriage also enjoyed steady employment in the North African and Italian campaigns. Faster and more maneuverable than the M7, it was a 75mm. howitzer mounted on an M5 light tank chassis.

Two half-track self-propelled guns were also used by the Allies in North Africa. They were the M15 which mounted an automatic 37mm. gun and two .50 cal. anti-aircraft machine guns; and the T19, an M3 half-track personnel carrier mounting a 105mm. howitzer.

TECHNICAL NOTES: The M12 Gun Motor Carriage had a combat weight of 27.1 tons, a top speed of 21 m.p.h., a 400 h.p. Wright nine cylinder radial engine, vertical volute suspension, 1-inch front and .4-inch side armor, one 155mm. gun M1917A1, and a five-man crew. The M40 weighed 40.5 tons, had a top speed of 24 m.p.h. and mounted a 155mm. M2 "Long Tom" gun.

The German Self-Propelled 75mm. Gun

AMONG THE MAJOR POWERS THAT ENGAGED IN WORLD WAR II, GERMANY was the first to build and employ self-propelled guns on a large scale. She designed and produced a wide assortment of these powerful mobile weapons based on her excellent PzKw II light, and PzKw III and IV medium tanks. In addition, her technicians adroitly improvised a number of others using armored vehicles captured from Poland, Czechosolvakia, Belgium, and France.

Used in many roles on all war fronts, German self-propelled guns were constructed on both tank and half-track chassis. They mounted high angle assault artillery, direct fire anti-tank guns, and anti-aircraft guns ranging in size from 37mm. to 150mm. All those based on the PzKw III series of tanks resembled one another. They were extremely mobile, low in silhouette, and presented difficult targets. One of the earliest to see action was the 75 StuK. It was composed of a short 75mm. gun mounted on a standard PzKw III tank chassis. An exceptionally low superstructure surrounded the gun which had considerable elevation, but was limited in traverse.

The 75 StuK was initially used in the campaign against Poland, and then in the invasion of the Low Countries and the Battle of France. Subsequently fitted with auxiliary armor which reached a thickness of four inches on frontal areas, it served with the Afrika Korps in Egypt and Tunisia, and on the eastern front against Russia.

Characterized by its stubby gun, which looked like a half-extended

One of Germany's best light SP guns was the 75mm. Stu. K40 gun mounted on the chassis of a PzKw III medium tank. This one has just been captured by U. S. troops in Italy.

The short barreled 75mm. gun mounted on a PzKw III chassis was known as the **Sturmgeschutz.** It was one of Germany's first war-time SP guns.

The PzKw III chassis was also used to mount a 105mm. howitzer.

pocket telescope and made the vehicle simple to identify, the 75 StuK was powered by a 265 h.p. gasoline engine. It moved on medium-width tracks at a maximum speed of 28 m.p.h. and had a range of approximately 100 miles.

Similar to the 75 StuK, but far more effective in combat because of a harder-hitting gun with greater range, was the self-propelled 75mm. high-velocity cannon. Also based on a PzKw III tank chassis, it was extensively employed as an anti-tank weapon against the British in North Africa. Heavily armored to begin with, the vehicle was later equipped with additional sheets of plate or wire mesh along its sides as protection against the American rocket-firing bazooka.

A little nomenclature might, at this point, help to suggest the variety and complexity of German SP weapons. Both of the vehicles described above were commonly called *Sturmgeschütz,* but the short-barreled version was categorized as an assault gun (*Sturmpanzer*) and the long-barreled, as a tank destroyer (*Jagdpanzer*). Other German SP categories included self-propelled anti-tank guns (*Panzerjäger*), SP anti-aircraft (*Panzerflak*), SP artillery (*Panzerinfanteriegeschütz, Panzerfeldhaubitze,* etc.) and so on. Over thirty distinct vehicles were included in these categories alone. In battle, of course, they were used as needed, and not merely for their formally designated purposes.

TECHNICAL NOTES: The 75mm. Self-Propelled Gun on a PzKw III light tank chassis had a combat weight of 25.6 tons, a top speed of 25 m.p.h., a 300 h.p. Maybach V-12 cylinder engine, synchromesh transmission, torsion bar suspension, 2-inch front armor supplemented with 1.2-inch plates and 1.2-inch side armor, one 75mm. gun K40, and a four-man crew.

German Heavy Self-Propelled Guns

THE FINAL YEAR OF THE WAR SAW A FANTASTIC PROLIFERATION OF German self-propelled artillery. As the Allies closed in on the shattered Reich a bewildering assortment of tracked guns emerged to do battle against the oncoming tide of Russian, British and American troops.

Even before this, wide-ranging German experiments in self-propelled weapons had done much to blur any orderly distinction between tanks, tank-destroyers and SP artillery. PzKw IV chassis, for example, were used to mount 88mm., 105mm. and 150mm. guns—all of which could be used as assault, support, or anti-tank weapons. 150mm. guns were also mounted on PzKw II chassis, French Lorraine chassis, and Czech PzKw 38 chassis. Tiger chassis appeared mounting 88mm. and 128mm. guns and a 380mm. rocket launcher. And so on and on.

A majority of these combinations were frankly lash-ups. The Czech PzKw 38 chassis, for example, was not standard *Wehrmacht* equipment, and most of the guns fitted on it made the lightly armored vehicle precariously top-heavy. Indeed, some of the guns were not even German. One version, used in the closing stages of the North African campaign and in Italy, carried captured Russian 76.2mm. high-velocity anti-tank guns mounted clumsily in a high-riding armored shield. But all of these weapons were dangerous opponents and some—those in which weapon and carrier were truly integrated—were terribly effective.

One such weapon was the Stu H-43, a PzKw IV chassis mounting a short-barreled 150mm. howitzer. Called "Grizzly Bear" by U. S. troops,

Typical of German heavy SP weapons was this big 150mm. howitzer mounted on a PzKw IV chassis. U. S. troops called the machine "Bumble Bee."

The Hunting Tiger (a 128mm. gun on a Tiger B chassis) weighed nearly 80 tons.

A short-barreled 105mm. howitzer mounted on a PzKw IV was called "Grizzly Bear" by U. S. troops. Note the armored skirting which protects the running gear.

The light Czech 38 chassis carried this German 75mm. PAK gun. The vehicle was used as a tank destroyer.

this was a pure assault weapon. Only half of the howitzer's stubby barrel protruded beyond the ball-mounting in the sloping front of an armored, low-slung superstructure. Protective steel plates hung over the bogies and return rollers: a defense against bazooka and conventional anti-tank fire. The "Grizzly Bear" was an efficient and destructive piece of mobile artillery, but was highly vulnerable to overhead high explosive bursts.

Equally efficient and rather better known was the Hunting Tiger. Actually a big 128mm. gun mounted on a Tiger chassis, the Hunting Tiger was used both as a tank destroyer and as an assault gun. No comparable British or American weapon existed and those Soviet SP's which *were* comparable were probably not as good. In the Hunting Tiger, the German tendency towards giganticism in tracked weapons reached a sort of climax; the gross weight of the machine even exceeded the 76.9 ton combat weight of the regular King Tiger heavy tank.

TECHNICAL NOTES: The Hunting Tiger self-propelled anti-tank/assault gun had a combat weight of 79 tons, a top speed of 26 m.p.h., a 700 h.p. Maybach V-12 cylinder engine, torsion bar suspension, preselective transmission, 5.9-inch front and 9.9-inch superstructure armor, one 128mm. gun PJK 80, one 7.9mm. machine gun, and a six-man crew. The 150mm. Self-Propelled Gun on a PzKw IV chassis had a combat weight of 25.4 tons, a top speed of 25 m.p.h., one 150mm. gun F.H. 18/1, one 7.9mm. machine gun and two 9mm. machine pistols.

Russian Self-Propelled Guns

THE RED ARMY PRODUCED ITS FIRST UNARMORED SELF-PROPELLED artillery in 1932. In the years which followed the Soviets showed the same kind of partiality for these weapons as the Germans, and during World War II they developed a large and impressive family of armored assault and support weapons.

In terms of employment the Russians tended to ignore their own theoretical distinction between assault and support weapons. Assault guns were intended to employ direct fire against centers of resistance, enemy tanks and artillery. They were supposed to follow Soviet infantry and tanks at a distance not greater than 400 yards. The support weapons, on the other hand, were intended merely to fulfill the normal support role of field artillery and anti-aircraft. In practice, the weapons often were used interchangeably.

One of the earliest war-time assault weapons was the standard 76.2mm. divisional gun mounted on the chassis of a T-40 light tank. Designated the SU-76, the weapon was originally intended as a tank destroyer, but it proved inadequtae for this and was eventually employed as a regimental support weapon.

The SU-85, a combination of the 85mm. anti-aircraft gun and a T-34 chassis, and the SU-100, a late-war combination of the 100mm. field gun and a T-34 chassis, were the Red Army's principal war-time tank destroyers. Unlike American TD's, neither mounted its guns in a revolving turret.

The largest assault gun in the Red Army was the JSU-152. This was a 152mm. M1937 gun-howitzer mounted on the chassis of a Stalin I or II. The same chassis and similar hulls were used to mount the 122mm. corps gun and the 122mm. AT gun.

The KV-II mounted a 152mm. howitzer in an enormous turret set on a KV chassis.

The SU-100 was a tank destroyer. It used the T-34 chassis to carry a 100mm. field gun.

One of the smaller Soviet SP guns was the SU-76, a 76.2mm. divisional gun carried on a T-70 light tank chassis.

The larger self-propelled weapons, the JSU-122 and JSU-152 were 122mm. guns and 152mm. gun-howitzers, respectively, mounted on JS-I and II Stalin tank chassis. They were formally called assault weapons but often doubled in the support role.

The only Soviet SP gun which was mounted in a revolving turret was a 152mm. howitzer placed on a KV heavy tank chassis. The turret of this ungainly weapon had a vertical dimension nearly as great as that of the hull itself. It looked a little like a disembodied portion of the main battery of a battleship as it rumbled across the Russian plains. In addition to being slow and clumsy, it was a well-nigh irresistible target for German gunners. Its use was discontinued in mid-war.

In typical Russian fashion, the Red Army employed its SP weapons on a massive scale. Great numbers of them assisted in the destruction of an estimated 1,500 German armored vehicles in the three-day battle of Kursk in mid-1943. They formed a large segment of the awesome 22,000-piece artillery concentration which laid siege to Berlin, and accompanied T-34's and Stalins in the bitter block-to-block fighting which followed the collapse of the German capital's outer defenses.

TECHNICAL NOTES: A good example of Soviet heavy self-propelled guns is the JSU-122 which had a combat weight of 51 tons, a top speed of 23 m.p.h., a 512 h.p. V-12 cylinder engine, one 122mm. gun M1931/44, one 12.7mm. machine gun, and a five-man crew. It was duplicated in every feature but main weapon by the JSU-152 which had a 152mm. gun M1937/43 with muzzle brake.

The Russian 76.2mm. Divisional Gun

FROM THE BEGINNING OF WORLD WAR II, THE EXCELLENCE OF RUSSIAN artillery was internationally acknowledged. Stalin regarded artillery as "the god of war," and saw to it that the Red Army was equipped accordingly. Artillery, in fact, comprised the greatest part of the strength of Soviet ground forces. Specifically, for every one thousand men, the Red Army had thirty to thirty-two artillery pieces.

One of the most widely used of Soviet field guns was the 76.2mm. M1942. In traditional wheel mount, it was profusely distributed in batteries throughout the army. Three batteries at least were included in the armament of each division. And another battery was coupled with one of 122mm. guns in every artillery regiment.

The 76.2mm. also was the main armament of the notable Soviet T-34 medium tanks during the first half of the war. Captured, the gun was made self-propelled by the Germans who mounted it on the chassis of the Czech TNHP (PzKw 38) light tank. In the great destructions of German tanks in the battles of Moscow, Stalingrad, and Kursk, the 76.2mm. typified the amazing scope and strength of Russian artillery.

The reason why the 76.2mm. gun was successful against German medium tanks was that it was sufficiently big and high-powered to deal with the improvements in tank armor which were made during the early war years. In the 1930's most of the major combatants had failed to foresee that such improvements would take place, and, as a result, most of the light anti-tank artillery which they had developed quickly became

The Germans used many captured Soviet weapons against the Allies. The British took this Russian 76.2mm. divisional gun from the Germans in North Africa.

The British 6-lb. gun had good mobility and a relatively high rate of fire but was not really a first-class anti-tank gun.

The German 50mm. anti-tank gun was one of the more successful smaller caliber AT weapons.

The U. S. 37mm. gun lacked the punch to make it a satisfactory AT gun.

obsolete. The Russians, with their 76.2mm. guns and the Germans, with their "88," were fortunate in having heavy-calibre alternatives to their 37mm., 50mm., and 57mm. weapons. The Western Allies were not so lucky.

The British 2-lb. gun and the American 37mm. gun were simply too small to be adequate AT weapons. They could do damage to treads but their shells usually bounced harmlessly off the turrets even of PzKw III's. The British had better luck with their 6-lb. gun, but it was never the equal of its Russian and German counterparts. Often the British and Americans had to fall back on the not-always satisfactory expedient of using standard artillery pieces as anti-tank weapons. Thus the British 25-lb. gun-howitzer, the American 3-inch gun, and the American 105-mm. howitzer were sometimes pressed into AT service.

TECHNICAL NOTES: The 76.2mm. Gun M1942, mounted on the 57mm. AT Gun carriage, weighed 1.2 tons, depressed five degrees, elevated 37 degrees, traversed 54 degrees, fired 25 rounds-per-minute a maximum range of 14,545 yards, and using high-velocity armor-piercing ammunition could penetrate 3.62 inches of armor at 550 yards.

The German 88mm. Gun

THE MAGNIFICENT GERMAN 88MM. GUN WAS, WITHOUT QUESTION, THE
single most famous artillery piece used in World War II. It was originally
designed as an anti-aircraft gun, and as such it remained without peer.
But its greatest, almost legendary, fame was won as an anti-tank weapon.
Actually there were eight "88's," developed and produced for anti-aircraft, assault, and direct fire anti-tank weapons between 1917 and 1944.

The "88" made its shocking debut as a tank killer in June, 1941,
when Rommel's headlong drive towards Egypt brought the Afrika Korps
to Halfaya Pass and precipitated the bloody Battle of Salum. From
superbly camouflaged emplacements, "88's" cut loose, at point blank
range, at an attacking British force of 238 heavy, medium and light
tanks. Taken by surprise and unable adequately to return fire, the British
lost 123 tanks—nearly two-thirds of them to the guns. The German gunners claimed one British tank for every twenty rounds fired at Halfaya
Pass, and at Capuzzo, a battery of eight "88's" alone accounted for 36
tanks.

The "88" could slam its 22-lb. shell through the heaviest British
armor at a distance of one mile. "It will prove the undoing of the Mark
II (medium tank)," remarked one gloomy British POW, and indeed, for
all practical purposes, it did. Until the advent of the American Shermans,
the British Eighth Army in Africa was largely at the mercy of the "88's"
and PzKw IV's; and the Sherman's armor was not proof against a direct
hit from an "88."

The German "88" was undoubtedly the most famous artillery
piece of World War II. Actually there were some eight variants
which succeeded the original 1917 design. Here, U. S. soldiers in
Germany test fire an 88mm. FLAK 36. The FLAK 36 was similar in
most respects to the basic FLAK 18.

The "88" was famous both as an anti-aircraft and an anti-tank weapon. Here a U. S. 90mm. AA gun (foreground) is compared with an "88" at the Aberdeen Proving Grounds.

This Soviet 57mm. AT gun, a 1943 design, was captured from the Chinese in Korea.

The Japanese often used their medium field artillery pieces as AT guns. This 77mm. gun was used against U. S. armor on Luzon in 1945.

Throughout the remainder of the war, the "88" remained unsurpassed as a conventional anti-tank gun. When mounted on the chassis of German medium and heavy tanks, it became one of the most deadly of self-propelled tank destroyers, and it provided the main armament for Germany's awesome Tiger tanks.

After the war some German officers observed that they could never understand why the British did not use their powerful 3.7-inch anti-aircraft gun like the "88" as an anti-tank weapon. Whatever the reason, the British relied primarily on their basic 6-lb. guns and 25-lb. gun-howitzers for heavy anti-tank artillery, and later in the war these were supplemented by the 17-lb. high-velocity tank gun.

At the outset, America possessed no heavy anti-tank artillery comparable to the "88," but the development of the bazooka, the 76mm. higher velocity tank gun and the 90mm. self-propelled gun eventually helped to close the gap.

The Russians had a variety of guns in a class with, but probably somewhat inferior to, the "88." In addition to the famous 76.2mm. gun, they used long-barrelled 85mm. dual-purpose anti-aircraft guns and 100-mm. field guns with great effect against German armor.

TECHNICAL NOTES: The basic multi-purpose 88mm. Gun Flak 18 in firing position weighed 5.5 tons, depressed three degrees, elevated 85 degrees, traversed 360 degrees, and fired 22-lb. projectiles at a rate of 15 to 20 per minute ranges of 11,501 yards (vertical) and 16,183 yards (horizontal). Three means of fire control equipped it for anti-aircraft fire (data transmission), anti-tank fire (direct laying), and indirect fire (indirect laying).

The British 25-Pound Gun-Howitzer

ON THE MOONLIT EVENING OF OCTOBER 23, 1942, AT QUARTER TO NINE, one of World War II's few truly large and prolonged artillery barrages initiated the third, final and greatest Battle of El Alamein between the British Eighth Army and Germany's much-vaunted Afrika Korps and Panzer Army Afrika, with its allied Italian forces.

Against the strongest section of the Axis front, a thousand British light, medium, and heavy artillery pieces, sitting thirty feet apart on a 10,000-yard stretch, ripped the stillness of the desert night to shreds with a thunderous roar. From high-angled barrels came a continuous hail of lethal metal for some twenty minutes in the initial stage of what later settled down to become five grueling hours of intermittent shelling. The Axis lines became a boiling strip of explosions, smoke and stinging, flying sand.

In this great wall of artillery were four hundred of one of the most dependable and widely used pieces of artillery employed by Britain, the 25-lb. gun-howitzer. The 25-pounder was used in concentration on every Allied front of the war, in North Africa, Italy, France, Burma, Malaya, throughout the Low Countries, and along the great northern front in the Battle of the Rhineland. At Cassino, 25-pounders belted out their shells by the score, hour after hour; at one point, there were so many of the guns in action their incessant fire ranged up and down the gun-line like machine gun chatter.

The 25-pounder was typical of the enormous group of howitzers and

The widely used British 25-lb. (87.6mm.) gun-howitzer was one of the great medium artillery pieces of the war. It had a maximum horizontal range of 12,500 yards. This picture shows the 25-pounder in action in New Guinea.

A British 4.5 inch gun in the Western Desert.

A German 105mm. howitzer—one of the **Wehrmacht's** standard pieces.

A U. S. 105mm. howitzer in Alaska, its wheels on wicker mats to keep it from sinking in the mud.

guns which fall under the general heading of light and medium field artillery. There were, in World War II, so many weapons belonging to this class (ranging from about 75mm. to 125mm.) that only a few examples can be listed here.

In addition to the 25-pounder, British field artillery made extensive use of both a 3.7-inch howitzer and a powerful 4.5-inch gun. American medium artillery weapons included a 75mm. howitzer, a 105mm. infantry howitzer, and an excellent 105mm. gun-howitzer.

Among the more familiar weapons in Germany's vast arsenal of field artillery were a short-barrelled 75mm. howitzer and the standard 105mm. howitzer and 105mm. gun. Russia's even larger arsenal included 76mm. howitzers, 85mm. and 100mm. guns, and 122mm. howitzers and guns. The Japanese favored mobility in their ordnance and thus preferred light weapons such as their 70mm. howitzer and 75mm. field gun. Early in the war they had made some use of a larger 120mm. howitzer, but this was gradually replaced by a newer and better 105mm. howitzer.

The naval equivalents of medium field artillery were the 4- to 6-inch guns which composed the main batteries of destroyers and the secondary batteries of battleships and cruisers. Typical was the U. S. Navy's 5-inch semi-automatic gun which fired a 54-lb. projectile a maximum horizontal distance of 18,000 yards. This gun had a maximum rate of fire of 22 rounds-per-minute and was occasionally used as an anti-aircraft weapon as well as a surface gun.

TECHNICAL NOTES: The 25-lb. Gun/Howitzer (87.6mm.) weighed 4,048 pounds in firing position, depressed five degrees, elevated 40 degrees, traversed eight degrees when wheel-mounted (360 degrees on platform), and fired four rounds-per-minute a maximum horizontal range of 12,500 yards, using high-explosive, armor-piercing or smoke ammunition.

The U. S. 155mm. Heavy Gun

IN 1940, THE ARTILLERY OF THE UNITED STATES ARMY CONSISTED OF approximately nine thousand light, medium, and heavy field pieces, not including a number of extra-large, unwieldly 8-inch railroad guns, nine of which saw action (although their worth had, to some extent, been proven in France during World War I). But, by July, 1945, for American ground forces and their allies, the nation's factories had produced nearly 600,000 pieces of artillery.

Of these, the great majority were light and medium calibre weapons, but the long-range high-powered "heavies" also played a vital role. One of the finest heavy guns turned out for Allied use, both as towed artillery and as a self-propelled weapon, was the U. S. 155mm. M2 Gun. Nicknamed the "Long Tom," it kicked a 95-pound projectile upwards of fifteen miles. The gun's accuracy was uncanny. Far behind enemy lines it could smash pill boxes and disrupt traffic as if firing point blank.

The "Long Tom" could be emplaced for action in as little time as one hour. Firing at the rate of 40 rounds an hour, it used separate-loading type ammunition—shell, propelling charge, and primer—and high-explosive, armor-piercing, chemical, smoke or illuminating shells. Its 23-foot barrel could be elevated a maximum sixty-five degrees either manually or by means of a fast-action hydraulic system. The gun was split-trailed, mounted on a ten-wheel rubber tired carriage and accompanied advancing troops behind a full-tracked prime mover.

In action, it was a highly reliable performer. Ranked side by side,

An American 155mm. M2 "Long Tom," its barrel in high elevation, guards the beach of a Pacific atoll.

U. S. soldiers in Italy inspect a wrecked German 170mm. gun.

A Russian 152mm. howitzer captured from the Germans by the U. S. 9th Army.

An American 155mm. howitzer cuts loose on Japanese positions on Luzon.

formations of 155mm. guns were the elite among the artillery which pounded the Japanese to defeat and surrender on Leyte during the liberation of the Philippines. At Anzio, one battalion of 155mm. guns alone fired 88,000 rounds in the course of breaking the deadlock which had developed following the Allied landings there in January, 1944. During an intense forty-eight-hour assault on the famous Siegfried Line, north of the Moselle, between Cologne and Coblenz, self-propelled 155mm. guns assisted in the obliteration of 120 pillboxes—removing one with each round fired at a range of three hundred yards.

The largest piece of towed artillery employed by the Germans on both European fronts, and in Italy, was the excellent 170mm. gun. Pivot-mounted on a box carriage, it fired a 150-pound projectile some sixteen miles, could punch through 3.5 inches of armor plate, and compared favorably with the giant 200mm. gun introduced by the United States late in the war.

For heavy artillery operations the British employed a 5.5-inch gun. A highly accurate and dependable piece, it was used in great numbers in the Rhineland offensive which followed the British drive through the Low Countries—an offensive which opened with the heaviest barrage laid down by British guns during the war. Its even larger howitzer counterpart was a massive 7.2-inch weapon which the British used effectively in Italy.

The Russians used three separate 152mm. weapons. The 152mm. gun had a range of 28,600 yards; the gun-howitzer, with characteristic split trail and muzzle brake, 18,900 yards; and the simple howitzer, 13,600 yards. Variations of these weapons appeared as SP guns on the JSU-152 and the monstrous KV-II.

TECHNICAL NOTES: The 155mm. Gun M2 weighed 15.1 tons over-all, depressed 1.8 degrees, elevated 63.3 degrees, traversed 30 degrees to right or left, and fired 40 rounds an hour or two rounds-per-minute in bursts, a maximum range of 25,715 yards.

Very Heavy Artillery

WORLD WAR II WAS THE MOST FLUID AND FAR-FLUNG OF WARS. EVERY-where the accent was on mobility. And this to some extent explains why ultra-heavy artillery was not more used. Although much was done to make them easier to move about on land, heavy guns firing projectiles larger than eight inches inevitably caused logistic problems.

Anglo-American use of ultra-heavy artillery, apart from naval ordnance, was confined primarily to the major campaigns. Thus, following the Normandy landings, 8-inch American howitzers, throwing their 240-lb. shells some ten and a half miles, were uncorked against the German garrison at Brest. Eight-inch and 240mm. howitzers and long-barrelled 8-inch guns pounded Hitler's last organized line of defense west of the Rhine.

Likewise, ultra-heavy howitzers were used against the Japanese on Luzon during the invasion of the Philippines. And the Japanese, for their part, replied with medium and heavy naval guns removed from warships and permanently installed around the Manila defense perimeter. One American company commander was prompted to remark, "Tell Bull Halsey to stop looking for the Jap fleet; it's dug in on Nichols Field."

On Germany's eastern front, Russia hammered towards the gates of Berlin in the wake of staggering bombardments from such weapons as 240 and 305mm. howitzers and 12- and 15.5-inch guns.

The main batteries of battleships provided the naval counterpart of

One of the two massive German 11-inch railroad guns which the Allies called the "Anzio Annie." An example of these 200-ton monsters is now on display at the Ordnance Museum, Aberdeen Proving Grounds, Maryland.

The Japanese mounted 5-inch naval guns around the Manila defense perimeter.

A big U. S. 240mm. howitzer being test-fired in a post-war demonstration.

A Russian 203mm. howitzer on a tracked carriage.

ultra-heavy field artillery. The big naval rifles were usually 14- to 16-inch pieces, although the two battleships of Japan's *Yamato* class carried 18-inchers. The great 16-inch guns which armed all of America's newer battlewagons were typical. Normally triple-mounted in large turrets, these guns used bag-type ammunition and hurled their more-than-one-ton projectiles about 25 miles.

Railroad guns had been used in World War I, but they were all but unknown during World War II. The most famous exceptions were the two 280mm. K-5E railroad guns which the Germans brought into play after the Anzio landing. Known as "Anzio Annies," the 200-ton monsters rained 550-pound shells on the advancing Allies with clockwork precision and successfully played hide-and-seek with the bombers sent out to destroy them. In the end, the great guns were only silenced when they were surrounded and captured. But by far the largest railroad guns to see service in the war were two gigantic 800mm. weapons developed by the Germans. Even "Anzio Annie" was dwarfed by comparison. One of these incredible cannons was used briefly at the siege of Sevastopol, but like some ponderous dinosaur in the twilight of the Mesozoic, the 800mm. gun had passed far beyond the limits of useful size. It is remembered as a bizarre curiosity rather than as a really effective weapon.

TECHNICAL NOTES: A typical big howitzer the U. S. 240mm. Howitzer weighed 25.5 tons over-all, elevated 15 to 65 degrees, traversed 22.5 degrees to right or left, and fired 30 rounds an hour or one round-per-minute rapid-fire for a maximum of 30 minutes, from 8,450 yards minimum to 25,225 yards maximum range. At the same rates, supercharged, the U. S. 8-inch Gun had a maximum range of 35,635 yards.

The Bofors 40mm. Anti-Aircraft Gun

LIKE OTHER CLASSES OF ARTILLERY, ANTI-AIRCRAFT GUNS ARE DESCRIBED as heavy, medium or light. And like other classes of artillery, the AA guns of World War II tended to get heavier and more powerful as the fighting progressed. Much of the "light" AA of 1939 was practically useless by 1943.

The United States was particularly deficient in light AA weapons when the war began. For fire at altitudes under 5,000 feet, the U. S. relied mainly on the .50 cal. machine gun and a rather inefficient 37mm. cannon. The British, French, Belgians, Danes, Poles, Swedes, Czechs, Finns, Spanish, Austrians, Hungarians and Yugoslavs had all adopted the superb Swedish Bofors 40mm. automatic gun in the late 30's, but for some obscure reason, the U. S. shortsightedly rejected it.

America's error became manifest during the fall of 1940 when Allied AA weapons were subjected to their first major trial by combat. A majority of the two thousand guns defending Britain during the Blitz were Bofors and they proved themselves far superior to any available lighter weapons. But even before the Battle of Britain, the United States had belatedly decided to adopt the gun for its own use.

From 1940 on, the Bofors was the standard Anglo-American light AA weapon. Both armies used the gun on a wheeled carriage with attached folding outriggers. Both navies used the Bofors mounted in shipboard gun tubs; and in the latter part of the war, the U. S. Navy employed them in a formidable, specially designed quadruple mount. Wher-

From a gun tub beside the flight deck of an **Essex** class carrier, a quadruple Bofors 40mm. mount fires at attacking Japanese aircraft.

British 2-lb. pom-poms fire from their tubs on H.M.S. **Illustrious.**

A German 37mm. light AA gun is inspected by an American G.I.

A U. S. Army Bofors emplacement beside "Dragon's teeth" in a captured segment of the Siegfried Line.

ever it was used—against V-1's over London, against *Kamikazes* in the Pacific or even against German tanks and fortifications on the ground—the Bofors performed splendidly.

The Bofors was fully automatic. As long as the firing pedal remained depressed and 4-round clips were fed into the breech, the Bofors would provide fast, saturating fire against low-flying aircraft. The gun had a full 360 degree traverse and an elevation arc of 90 degrees, so that it could swivel and track its target without interruption.

A smaller calibre weapon greatly favored by the U. S. Navy was an adaptation of the Swiss Oerlikon 20mm. cannon often used in aircraft. The Navy employed vast quantities of these rapid-fire little guns, usually in single mounts, in preference to the .50 cal. AA machine gun.

The British Navy's equivalent of the Oerlikon was the Pom-Pom: rapid-fire 2-lb. guns in large multiple mounts. A similar Japanese 25mm. gun was used in triple mounts. Germany used a variant of the Oerlikon, as well as machine guns and an excellent Rheinmetall 37mm. gun. The Russians used a 37mm. Bofors.

TECHNICAL NOTES: The Bofors 40mm. Anti-Aircraft Gun in wheel-mount with outriggers weighed 5,850 pounds, depressed six degrees (11 degrees with jacks), elevated 90 degrees, traversed 360 degrees, and fired 120 rounds-per-minute automatically from 4-round clips a maximum range of 5,100 yards (vertical) and 5,200 yards (horizontal), range being limited by the self-destroying property of the standard tracer round.

The U. S. 90mm. Anti-Aircraft Gun

FLAK IS GERMAN NOMENCLATURE AND FLAK WAS A GERMAN SPECIALTY. Germany's anti-aircraft defenses, especially against aircraft flying at medium and high altitudes, were incomparably the best of the war. Even though the Germans never really believed that they would be subjected to heavy aerial bombardment, they entered the war prepared with one of the finest heavy anti-aircraft weapons of all time: the original 88mm. gun (which has been described elsewhere as an AT weapon).

Supplemented by the even larger 128mm. gun, which hurled big 35-lb. shells up to very high altitudes, massed batteries of "88's" made daylight raids over Germany living nightmares for Allied bomber pilots. They were a factor in bringing bomber losses to such frightful levels that the whole concept of daylight bombing was, for a time, brought into doubt.

By contrast, American heavy anti-aircraft artillery, at the beginning of the war, was in poor shape. The standard U. S. heavy AA weapon at that time was a 3-inch gun whose effective vertical range was only a little over 10,000 feet and whose rate of fire and accuracy left much to be desired. In 1940, however, the U. S. Army accepted the design for an improved 90mm. gun and within two years these weapons were rolling out of American factories at the rate of 2,000 a month.

The 90mm. gun was probably not the equal of the "88," but it was adequate for most purposes and it was much better than the 3-inch gun. The 90mm. could traverse 360 degrees and could elevate to a near-

An American 90mm. anti-aircraft gun overlooking a harbor in the Ryukus.

The British 3.7-inch gun was one of the best heavy AA weapons.

The big German 128mm. AA gun was a formidable weapon when used against high-altitude Allied bombers.

A German "88" in high elevation.

vertical position. It fired a 21-lb. shell a maximum 13,500 yards, although its effective range was considerably less. Loaded by an automatic rammer, the 90mm. could fire approximately 28 rounds per minute. At Anzio, London and various places in the Pacific, the 90mm's managed to run up some very impressive scores of enemy aircraft destroyed, particularly with proximity-fused ammunition.

The British equivalent of the 90mm. was the 3.7-inch gun, a formidable weapon which may have been marginally superior to its American counterpart. Twenty batteries of 90mm.'s firing proximity-fused shells combined with British 3.7-inchers and Bofors in defending London against the V-1's. Among them, they accounted for 438 of the jet-propelled bombs.

The standard Russian AA gun was an 85mm. weapon whose potential effectiveness was never fully realized due to the low quality of Russian fire-control. Like the German "88," it was also used as both a tank gun and an SP artillery weapon.

At the end of the war, the United States developed a first-class 120mm. gun capable of firing 12 to 15 projectiles per minute up to a maximum altitude of 60,000 feet. The war ended, however, before this fine gun had a chance to see any significant service.

TECHNICAL NOTES: The 90mm. Anti-Aircraft Gun mounted on outrigger platform weighed 2,370 pounds, elevated 90 degrees, traversed 360 degrees, and fired 23 to 28 rounds-per-minute maximum ranges of 13,500 yards (vertical) and 21,000 yards (horizontal). The 120mm. AA Gun fired a 50-lb. high-explosive projectile an effective vertical range of 16,000 yards, a maximum range of 20,000 yards (vertical) and 28,000 yards (horizontal).

The Japanese 50mm. "Knee Mortar"

MORTARS ARE AN ARMY'S MOST MANEUVERABLE FORM OF ARTILLERY. Small, lightweight smooth-bore mortars were used extensively by Axis and Allied infantry alike for short range offensive fire against enemy troop concentrations, entrenchments, machine gun nests, artillery emplacements and other definitely located targets in every theater of the war. Fast, handy and accurate, light mortars were especially useful in close combat on rough terrain, in the mountains and in woods and jungle.

One of the lightest and simplest small mortars introduced for infantry use was the Japanese 50mm. The American troops, against whom it was used in great numbers in the slow, tedious island jungle fighting that characterized land combat in the Pacific war, called this weapon the "knee mortar." This nickname derived from the mistaken belief the mortar was fired while braced against the operator's thigh, just above the knee. A round-ended concave base plate appeared to substantiate this explanation of operation, but when an American GI attempted to test-fire one of the mortars in this fashion, its recoil broke his leg.

Extremely simple in design, the 50mm. "knee mortar" provided the Japanese infantryman with greater firepower than a grenade launcher, but was actually closer to that weapon in type than to a true mortar. It fired a fused projectile resembling a present-day aerosol insect bomb to a maximum range of about 700 yards.

The most portable mortar employed by United States infantry during World War II was the 60mm. It weighed forty-five pounds. However,

The Japanese 50mm. "Knee Mortar" was neither a mortar (it was really a grenade launcher) nor a weapon which could be operated from the knee—as this G.I. would painfully discover if he were to fire it.

American soldiers examine a small German 50mm. mortar.

This U. S. 60mm. mortar is about to be fired at an enemy hill position in Italy.

later fitted with a smaller base plate, its weight was cut to twenty pounds, a refinement which made it possible for one man to fire the mortar as a hand-held weapon.

The American 60mm. mortar was smooth-bore, and fired a 3-lb. shell—stabilized in flight by fins—1,600 to 2,000 yards. Its sustained rate of fire was 18 rounds-per-minute, but a skilled operator was able to get off up to 30 rounds-per-minute. Both high-explosive and smoke ammunition were used in the mortar, the latter often to set up a screen for advancing tank-supported infantry.

Like Japan, Germany and Russia both equipped their infantry with light, portable 50mm. mortars. Both used the weapons in close combat at ranges of 100 yards and less. Germany also used a 50mm. mortar which was operated by remote control. Dozens were installed in the pillboxes of the Siegfried Line.

TECHNICAL NOTES: The U. S. 60mm. Mortar weighed 20 or 45 pounds depending on baseplate, elevated 45 to 85 degrees, and fired 3-lb. projectiles at rates of 18 rounds-per-minute sustained or 30 rounds-per-minute maximum rapid-fire to ranges of from 1,600 to 2,000 yards. The Japanese 50mm. grenade launcher could fire smoke grenades or demolition bombs weighing about 2 lbs. about 700 yds. at a rate of 18-20 r.p.m.

The U. S. 4.2-Inch Mortar

MEDIUM AND HEAVY MORTARS CAME TO PLAY EXTREMELY IMPORTANT roles in the long, intense engagements of infantry and armor comprising the giant Allied offensives which crushed the German military machine in Italy, Western Europe, Poland, Austria, Czechosolvakia and, eventually, within the heart of the Third Reich itself.

The medium U. S. 4.2-inch mortar made a tremendously effective showing in Italy and throughout the fighting which followed the landings in France in 1944. The weapon was known to its users as the "goon gun." Its mobility, punch, and versatility made the mortar a major addition to American artillery, and one of the infantry's favorite support weapons.

The 4.2-inch mortar was originally developed by the U. S. Army's Chemical Warfare Service to fire gas shells, but when common consent on both sides outlawed that hellish weapon of World War I, the mortar quickly found work hurling high explosives, white phosphorus, and smoke projectiles.

In effect a powerful muzzle-loading cannon, the mortar had a five-foot steel barrel, rifled for greater accuracy, and kicked a 24-pound flat-bottomed shell up to 4,500 yards in 60 seconds. Skilled crews were able to send as many as seven shells twisting into the air before the first one fired reached its target. In Italy, until they learned what weapon was being used, the rapid fire of the mortar had German troops convinced it was an automatic cannon. Also, it was during the fighting in Italy that a

Soldiers of the U. S. 7th Army in France fire a 4.2-inch mortar. Like all mortars, the 4.2-incher was useful in providing high-angle fire into defiladed areas.

A U. S. 81mm. mortar in the midst of a ruined German town.

German paratroopers with an 81mm. mortar fire on a Russian strong point. The weapon had a range of 2,078 yards.

An American soldier in Italy examines a Russian 120mm. mortar captured from the Germans.

4.2-inch mortar scored a hole-in-one. With phenomenal precision, it lobbed a high-explosive shell up, over, and straight down into a German tank through its open turret hatch. On another occasion, a dozen well-aimed rounds destroyed a battery of Germany's famous 88mm. guns in less than three minutes.

In addition to the 4.2-inch mortar, American troops also used the smooth-bore 81mm. mortar to great advantage. Easy to set up, it consisted of a 51-inch barrel, a bipod, and a base plate, and was operated by a three-man crew. Firing finned high-explosive shells like the smaller, lighter 60mm. mortar, hundreds of the 81mm. were used in the Battle of the Rhineland to help neutralize Germany's great west wall of fortifications.

Great numbers of mortars were also employed against Germany's eastern front by the Red Army. Some of its mortars ran as high as 305mm., but normally the Red Army used 50mm., 82mm. and 120mm. mortars in vast array with rocket projectors and a corresponding variety of towed and self-propelled artillery. Within every Soviet artillery regiment, in fact, was included a brigade of one hundred and eight 120mm. mortars.

TECHNICAL NOTES: The 4.2-inch Mortar with base plate and ring, rotator, bridge, standard, and sighting equipment 629 pounds, elevated approximately 45 to 60 degrees, traversed 360 degrees, and fired five rounds-per-minute sustained or 20 round-per-minute maximum rapid-fire a maximum range of 6,000 yards.

The Russian Katyusha Rocket Launcher

ABOUT THREE MONTHS AFTER THE GERMAN INVASION OF RUSSIA, THE ingenuity of Russian ordnance technicians was startlingly revealed by the introduction of a new and devastating weapon which the Germans called the "Stalin organ" and the Russians "Katyusha."

"Katyusha" was a general term used to designate a whole series of simple recoilless multiple rocket launchers. They consisted of nothing more than metal racks in which were placed as many as 36 rockets ranging in size from approximately 75mm. to 16 inches. What these fused projectiles lacked in accuracy (a good deal), they made up in pyrotechnic and sound effects.

The German troops who first experienced "Katyusha" bombardment were preparing for an attack. When suddenly the rockets began to howl down upon them, they simply turned and fled. Nor was the effect of the rockets merely psychological. The Russians claimed 17 tanks and 15 artillery pieces knocked out in the action.

Rocket launchers of the "Katyusha" type were quickly adopted by all the major combatants. They were crude and inaccurate, to be sure, but they provided ground forces with an inexpensive mobile form of artillery which could be used for area-saturation bombardment either before an attack or to break up an impending enemy attack.

A representative adaptation of the simple rocket launcher was the U. S. Army's standard 4.5-inch weapon. This consisted of any number of plywood tubes, each of which launched a 38-lb. missile with the de-

Russian Katyusha's—in this case, M-13 132mm. rocket launchers —fire on Japanese positions in Manchuria in 1945. The truck-mounted M-13 consisted of 16 rockets fired from eight rails.

A 60-tube American 4.5-inch rocket launcher. The tubes were made of plywood and had to be replaced after a few rounds were fired.

British anti-aircraft rocket launchers in North Africa in 1944.

Soviet M-13 rocket launchers on parade.

structive effect of a 105mm. shell about 4,400 yards. The 60-tube racks which were mounted atop the turrets of some Sherman tanks could launch all their projectiles within 30 seconds, after which the whole launcher could be jettisoned. Infantry and naval versions were also much used.

The 4.5-inch launcher was only a slight improvement over earlier Russian and German models, but everywhere the trend was toward greater sophistication and complexity. Late-war American experiments in recoilless artillery—stemming from experience with the 4.5 launcher and the bazooka, though different in principle—produced the excellent 75-mm. recoilless cannon which was used with good effect in Korea five years after the end of World War II.

TECHNICAL NOTES: Typical of the wide variety of Katyusha's, the 132mm. Rocket Launcher M13, truck-mounted, weighed 7.1 tons, elevated 15 to 45 degrees, traversed 10 to 20 dgrees on mount, and fired sixteen 94-pound rockets (ignited by electric impulse) a maximum range of 9,846 yards.

The German Nebelwerfer

IN THE GERMAN WEHRMACHT, THE TERM NEBELWERFER ORIGINALLY referred to any mortar which fired chemical or smoke shells. But to Allied soldiers in Europe during the later part of the war, the word had a more specific and considerably more alarming connotation. For the six-barreled 150mm. *Nebelwerfer* 41 was a rocket launcher—one of the most effective and most sophisticated pieces of rocket artillery used in the war.

Both the *Nebelwerfer* 41 and its five-barreled 210mm. successor were wheeled and were towed by ¾ tracks. Early in the war, their shell loadings were changed from chemical to H.E. and incendiary. According to one Allied observer at Cassino, where the *Nebelwerfer* was first used in large numbers, and where it quickly earned prominence and respect, its cluster of rockets made a sound while in flight that was a nerve-fraying cross between a shriek and a whine. Bass in timbre, it was not unlike the dreadful self-announcement emitted by the V-1 robot bomb as it soared to its target.

The German stand against the Allies at Cassino, following the breakout from Salerno, was one of the war's most tenacious. Field Marshal Kesselring directed a skillful, bitterly determined effort to maintain the Axis battleline between Gaeta, Cassino, and a parallel point south of Pescara. At Cassino, *Nebelwerfer*'s were virtually embedded in strategic emplacements hewn out of the hillside. In concert, several regiments of them literally rained death on the combination of British, American,

A six-barreled 150mm. German **Nebelwerfer** 41 captured in Tunisia. Unlike earlier weapons of the same name, this was a true rocket launcher.

A Japanese 8-inch rocket launcher captured on Luzon.

The late-war U. S. 75mm. recoilless gun was not a rocket launcher, even though it resembled one. The Germans used recoilless guns as early as the Battle of El Alamein.

French, and Polish troops that laid siege to the ancient monastery and its town.

The *Nebelwerfer* also played an important defensive role in the opening stages of the struggle to liberate occupied Europe. Beyond Caen, in France, comprising part of the highly organized, complex German defenses laid out by Rommel east of the Orne River, 272 of the powerful rocket-mortars were dug in. They gave the Germans 1,632 barrels from which they could unleash a drenching torrent on advancing Allied infantry between the Orne and the Dives.

In addition to rocket launchers, the Germans also experimented with recoilless guns—a type of artillery which was to become increasingly important in the post-war years. Unlike the rocket launcher, a recoilless weapon which fires a self-propelled projectile, the recoilless gun fires a conventional shell. The German 75mm. model, designed for potential use by paratroops, was typical. An open tube extended back from the breech. Gasses and the plastic base of the cartridge case blew backwards out the tube when the propellant charge burst, while the 2.5-lb. shell was hurled forward out the barrel to a maximum range of 7,400 yards. 75mm. and 105mm. recoilless pieces were used at El Alamein and later a 150mm. gun was also used in France. Although the U. S. Army did not begin to receive recoilless guns until very late in the war, they were generally superior to the most advanced German models.

TECHNICAL NOTES: The 150mm. Nebelwerfer 41 Rocket Projector, wheel-mounted, weighed 1,195 pounds, had six 51-inch long barrels, was fired electrically by remote control at a rate of six rounds every 90 seconds, and ranges of 2,710 yards at 6.5 degrees' elevation, 7,018 yards at 30 degrees, and 7,723 yards at 45 degrees, had a traverse of 30 degrees.

ARTILLERY

SMALL ARMS

THERE IS A POINT AT WHICH UBIQUITY MERGES INTO ANONYMITY. THIS IS one of the problems in trying to assess the role of small arms in the war. The basic tools of the infantry, huge quantities of them were constantly in action on every battlefront. Yet it is nearly impossible to say specifically what importance this or that rifle or machine gun may have had in a given action.

Nevertheless certain technological generalizations can be made about war-time small arms. Perhaps the most obvious concerns the trend towards increased fire-power for standard infantry units and, even more, for special-mission groups such as paratroops and commandos. This was accomplished, sometimes at the expense of accuracy, by the widespread introduction of automatic and semi-automatic shoulder weapons, by increased cyclic rates in standard machine guns and by the use of bazooka-type rocket launchers.

The Red Army went farthest in its emphasis on so-called assault and area fire by infantry. Submachine guns were issued wholesale, largely replacing rifles as the standard infantry weapon. The effect of this was to give Soviet ground troops a tremendous volume of fire which was, however, accurate only at comparatively short ranges.

Other armies were more conservative. The British, Germans, Japanese and Italians, in varying degrees, clung to the standard bolt-action rifle, with its low rate of fire and great range and accuracy, supplemented by machine guns. The Americans compromised on the excellent fast-firing Garand semi-automatic rifle, supplemented by a variety of automatic weapons and machine guns. Each arrangement had its partisans, although the American systems seem to have had fewer defects than most.

The U. S. 2.36-Inch Anti-Tank Rocket Launcher

A SUPERB AMERICAN ADAPTATION OF A PRINCIPLE USED BY THE CHINESE in battle more than a thousand years ago, the U. S. 2.36-inch anti-tank rocket launcher made its combat debut in Tunisia following the American landings in North Africa in the fall of 1943. U. S. troops took one look at the all-barrel brainstorm of stateside ordnance and immediately christened it "the bazooka," in honor of the bizarre gas pipe horn made famous by the late Bob Burns.

The bazooka provided the foot-soldier with a powerful, hard-hitting defensive weapon against the tank. Actually, it was no more than a section of metal tube, open at both ends, fitted with hand grips, a wooden shoulder stock, a breech guard, and a dry cell battery electrical set-up for igniting the rockets it fired. A sight was welded on the tube near the muzzle, and was equipped with four studs used in aiming the bazooka at ranges of 100, 200, 300, and 400 yards. The weapon was generally operated by a two-man team, one loading, the other aiming and firing.

The rocket fired by the bazooka weighed approximately three and a half pounds and carried a charge of high explosive which detonated upon contact. It was driven by a charge of powder ignited by the electrical system of the launcher, and was capable of penetrating heavy armor.

After the bazooka was introduced against the Panzer Army Afrika, Germany began fitting some of her PzKw IV tanks with heavy wire mesh side screens in an attempt to protect them against bazookas. A later ex-

The modern successor to the original bazooka is the 3.5-inch rocket launcher. This one was demonstrated at Fort Benning, Georgia, in 1949.

The German 88mm. rocket launcher was twice as powerful as the American 2.36-inch bazooka. Here some G.I.s in France test-fire the German weapon.

The American 57mm. recoilless rifle resembled the bazooka rocket launcher but actually operated on a different principle. It was developed too late to be used in World War II but saw action in Korea.

pedient was to place solid metal "skirts" over the tanks' vulnerable bogies.

The bazooka delivered an extremely powerful punch. It fired without recoil, which permitted the use of special kinds of high explosives in the warheads of its projectiles. In fact, the detonation of a bazooka rocket was so devastating, German tank commanders captured in the course of Allied armor and infantry advances across France after D-day expressed the belief they had been fired on by 155mm. guns at close range when the rockets struck near their vehicles.

Hard upon the bazooka, Germany came up with similar weapons of her own, the 88mm. *Raketenwerfer*. Her troops also used the bazooka itself after capturing numbers of them from the Russians who were supplied the rocket launchers under Lend-Lease.

It was the bazooka which paved the way for the U. S. 3.5-inch rocket launcher which fires a projectile able to pierce up to 11 inches of armor, and the small, handy M18 57mm. recoilless rifle (not, however, a rocket launcher), developed shortly after the war.

TECHNICAL NOTES: The 2.36-inch Anti-Tank Rocket Launcher M1 weighed approximately 12 pounds, was 54 inches in length, breech loading, electric impulse fired, and could be sight-aimed for fire at ranges of 100, 200, 300, and 400 yards.

The Russian 14.5mm. Anti-Tank Rifle

ANTI-TANK RIFLES, AS A CLASS (AND AS DISTINCT FROM WEAPONS LIKE the bazooka), were not a great success. They were originally conceived as portable infantry weapons which could perform the same functions as light anti-tank artillery. But since light artillery was itself becoming ineffective against the increasing toughness of war-time tank armor, the less powerful rifles could not hope to succeed. Nevertheless, anti-tank rifles did have their moments and many of the weapons used in the war still retain a certain amount of interest for weapons enthusiasts.

One of the few anti-tank "rifles" that actually looked anything like a rifle was the Russian Simonov 14.5mm. gun. But at best the resemblance was slight. The 14.5mm. looked a little like an old Kentucky squirrel gun and a little like a piece of discarded plumbing. Its construction was simple even by Russian standards. It was a single-shot, bolt-action affair measuring approximately seven feet from shoulder stock to muzzle brake. A bipod steadied the barrel while one man operated the rifle and another handed him armor-piercing high-explosive shells. Primitive as it was, the 14.5mm. rifle was crudely effective; it could punch through 1.2 inches of armor plate at 500 yards and could do considerable damage to the running gear of almost any tank. The Russians, of course, claimed many successes for the weapon, and it is still used today by Chinese and North Korean forces.

The German Guerlich 20mm. gun neither looked like a rifle nor was it simple. Indeed, it could probably be appropriately classed as light

A pair of Russian soldiers fire a Simonov single-action single-shot 14.5mm. AT rifle at a German PzKw III tank.

A Japanese 20mm. AT rifle.

A Tommy of the London Irish Rifles loads a P1AT.

This German Guerlich AT gun reduced a 28mm. shell to 20mm. in a tapered barrel. Other Guerlich guns were 47mm./28mm. and 75mm./55mm.

artillery since it was relatively large and was often mounted on a wheeled split-trail carriage. The odd thing about the Guerlich was that the bore of its barrel tapered from 28mm. at the breech to 20mm. at the muzzle. Its shells were ringed with soft iron bands which were actually compressed 8mm. as the shell traveled down the barrel. The pressure built up behind these gastight metal skirts "squeezed" the shell out of the gun at a maximum 4,400 feet per second. The Guerlich was used with some effect against light British tanks in North Africa.

Most other AT rifles were more conventional. Typical was the Japanese 20mm. automatic gun which was fired from the shoulder off a bipod and was fed from an 8-round clip. The Germans and the Italians used similar weapons.

One of the most genuinely effective AT weapons was the British PIAT (Projector Infantry Anti-Tank). This was a sort of cross between an anti-tank rifle and a bazooka. It fired a rocket-propelled charge but was not, by any means, a recoilless weapon. One Tommy in Italy who fired his PIAT at a Panther from a standing—rather than from the prescribed prone—position was knocked flat by the gun's kick (but he got the Panther and saved his company in the bargain). At short ranges the PIAT's 3-lb. projectile could pierce 4-inch armor. In terms of application, magnitude of use and general effectiveness, the PIAT's were equivalent to the U. S. and German bazookas.

TECHNICAL NOTES: The Simonov 14.5mm. Anti-Tank Rifle was approximately seven feet long overall, was bolt-action and fired one round of armor-piercing high-explosive ammunition. At a range of 500 yards it could penetrate 1.2 inches of armor plate. A lighter .60 cal. M1941 Degtyarov AT Rifle penetrated 1.2 inches of armor at 300 yards. Both these and the similar German PzB38 and PzB39 rifles were patterned on a Polish Mareszek AT rifle of 1935.

The U. S. Browning .50 M2 Heavy Machine Gun

IN WORLD WAR I IT HAD BEEN DEMONSTRATED THAT HEAVY MACHINE guns could be effective as anti-tank weapons. But by 1939 most tank armor had become thick enough to be proof against even the largest machine guns (those firing bullets approximately a half inch in diameter), and a majority of the great powers lost interest in the big guns.

The outstanding exception to this was the United States. America enthusiastically employed its heavy Browning .50 cal. M2 in all the ways other countries used their standard rifle calibre machine guns. The Army made the M2 a basic defensive weapon for the infantry. The armored forces used the M2 extensively as secondary armament in combat vehicles. All the services used the M2 as a light anti-aircraft weapon. And both the Army and Navy Air Forces used versions of the gun almost to the exclusion of any other rapid-fire weapon (American airmen scorned the smaller calibre machine guns carried by foreign planes and even insisted that the Browning was superior to the 20mm. aerial cannon). In all, some two million M2's were produced during the war.

There were persuasive arguments in favor of America's fondness for the M2. It had many of the good points of standard smaller calibre guns, plus great range, high accuracy and the brutal, shattering impact of its big bullets. It cycled at about 450 rounds per minute, had a maximum range of 7,200 yards, and had a muzzle velocity of 2,660 feet-per-second. In the air, the standard U. S. fighter armament of six M2's made a devastating crossfire which few enemy planes could sustain for more than a few seconds without falling to pieces.

U. S. soldiers of the 9th Army man a big Browning .50 cal. (M2) machine gun during the invasion of Germany.

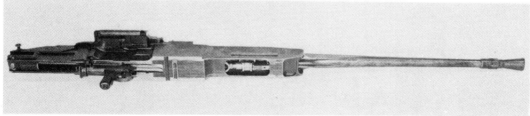

The Russian D. Sh. K. 12.7mm. machine gun was often mounted on a small wheeled carriage.

The British 15mm. Besa machine gun was usually mounted on tanks.

The British counterpart of the M2 was the 15mm. Besa machine gun. This massive, excellent weapon was little used save as secondary armament on armored vehicles. Since the Besa was originally a Czech design, a similar version of the gun appeared on some German tanks as well.

The standard Russian "heavy" was the 12.7mm. D.Sh.K. M1938. Like the M2, it is still in service—now primarily on armored vehicles. It was a simple sturdy weapon with good all-around characteristics, but was not nearly so widely used as the Browning. In the version assigned to the infantry, the M1938 was shielded and mounted on a small wheeled trailer which made the gun look something like a miniature artillery piece. The M1938 was air-cooled, as were most versions of the M2, and the barrel could be replaced with relative ease. Some Russian fighter planes, such as the YAK-3, also used a 12.7mm. Beresin aircraft machine gun but the more usual armament was a combination of 7.62mm. machine guns and 20mm. cannon.

TECHNICAL NOTES: The Browning .50 cal. Model HB M2 Heavy Machine Gun in field mount and on tanks weighed 81 pounds (anti-aircraft mount 121.5 pounds), had a 36- or 45-inch air-cooled barrel, a cyclic rate of fire of 400 to 500 rounds-per-minute, telescopic sight, spade-grip trigger, and a maximum range of 7,200 yards. Ammunition was belt fed from 100-round belts.

The British Vickers .303 Machine Gun

THERE IS A CERTAIN AMOUNT OF CONFUSION ABOUT WHAT CONSTITUTES a "heavy" machine gun. Any tripod-mounted defensive machine gun, especially if it happens to be liquid-cooled, will be weighty enough, but such a weapon may not necessarily fire large-calibre bullets. On the whole it is simpler to talk about "standard rifle calibre" machine guns when one intends defensive guns in the .30 cal. range.

Nearly all the World War II combatants used such weapons extensively, and most had generally similar characteristics. It is perhaps gratuitous to single out one design from the rest, but certainly no machine gun was more famous and few were more widely used than Britain's reliable old Vickers .303-inch (*i.e.* .303 cal.).

An early design, adopted in 1912, and based on an older U. S. Maxim, the belt-fed Vickers was still a standard infantry and aircraft weapon in the Second World War. Liquid cooled, with a cycling rate of about 500 r.p.m., it was extensively copied by the weapons manufacturers of other nations.

The American counterpart of the Vickers was the Browning .30 cal. Both air- and liquid-cooled versions of the gun were extensively used by the infantry, and the lighter air-cooled version was used by the Navy and the armored forces as well. In the first half of the war, a British version of the gun, the Browning .303-inch MK II, comprised the standard fixed armament in British fighter planes (the Vickers was more used in turrets and on flexible mounts). It was thus the Browning .303 which

Adopted by the British Army in 1912, the Vickers .303 cal. machine gun was based on the old U. S. Maxim design.

An American Browning .30 cal. (liquid cooled version) machine gun in position on an Italian hillside.

Japanese infantrymen firing a 7.7mm. machine gun at enemy troop positions. The weapon was a copy of the French Hotchkiss.

U. S. soldiers in Korea examine two Russian machine guns. In the foreground, the Goryunov M1943 7.62mm.; behind, the Maxim M1910 7.62mm.

rode to glory in the wings of Spitfires and Hurricanes during the grim autumn of 1940.

The Germans made some use of standard 7.92mm. rifle-calibre machine guns during the war, but German tactical doctrine emphasized offensive operations, and light machine guns, because of their greater mobility, were generally preferred.

The Russian standard rifle-calibre weapon was the excellent original Maxim and later the Goryunov 7.62mm. M1943. This belt-fed Goryunov was a gas-operated machine gun and fired the 7.62mm. M1930 round with good accuracy at a fairly high cyclic rate. It was a considerable improvement over the stolid old Maxim 7.62mm. M1910, which it replaced during the middle war years. The Red Army still uses the Goryunov as a substitute standard infantry and tank weapon, and both the Goryunov and the Maxim are used by the Chinese.

The Japanese standard machine gun was the 7.7mm. Model 92, a modified version of the famous French Hotchkiss. It used semi-rimmed cartridges, cycled at about 450 r.p.m. and had a muzzle velocity of about 2,400 feet-per-second. Unlike most comparable machine guns, which were belt-fed, this weapon accepted cartridges from a semi-rigid strip containing 30 bullets.

TECHNICAL NOTES: The Vickers .303-inch Machine Gun weighed 33 pounds with water jacket empty (43 pounds when full), had a 24.5-inch barrel, a cyclic rate of fire of 500 rounds-per-minute, calibrated leaf rear and blade front sights, spade-grip trigger, and an accurate range of 600 yards (effective and maximum ranges much greater).

The German 7.92mm. MG42 Light Machine Gun

LIGHT MACHINE GUNS—AT LEAST IN THE CONTEXT OF THIS BOOK— comprise a category of rapid-fire rifle-calibre weapons distinguished by light weight and an adaptability for both offensive and defensive operations. Some of the most famous small arms used in the war belong to this class.

Best of all the light machine guns used in World War II was probably the German 7.92mm. MG42. A replacement for the fine MG34 with which Germany began the war, the MG42 first went into action at Bir Hacheim when members of the Afrika Korps, returning from leave in Germany, brought examples of the weapon back to North Africa.

The MG42 was fired like a rifle, its barrel braced on a simple bipod mount. Belt-fed and recoil-operated, the gun had a fantastic maximum cycling rate of 1,200 rounds per minute and a maximum range of about 4,000 yards. It was easily portable and was simple to mass-produce.

Technically less impressive but potent nonetheless, was the famous British Bren .303-inch, a pre-war refinement of an original Czech design. The Bren could be fired from a prone position, using a bipod, or from the hip. Like the MG42, it doubled as an infantry weapon and as an anti-aircraft gun and was, in addition, used on some armored vehicles. It cycled at about 500 r.p.m. and was fed by a curved 30-round clip mounted atop the breech.

Equally famous were the standard Russian Degtyarov DP and

This war-time display shows the MG 42 and the MG 34 (center). The Schmeisser MP 38 (lower left) is described in the next section and the rifles (top) are discussed on pages 315 and 319. The 7.92mm. MP 44 (lower right) is incorrectly labeled and described in the display.

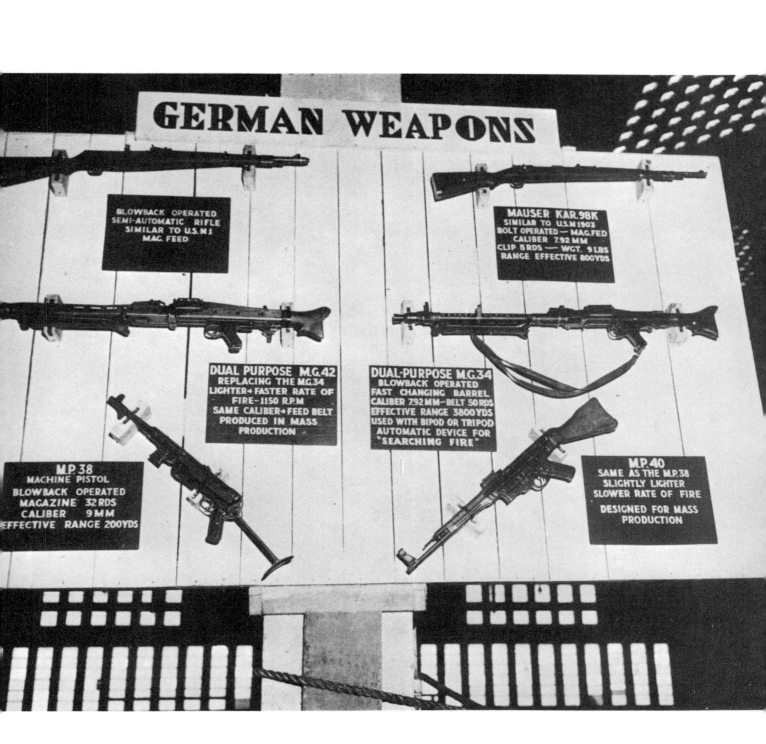

GERMAN WEAPONS

**BLOWBACK OPERATED
SEMI-AUTOMATIC RIFLE
SIMILAR TO U.S.M 1
MAG. FEED**

**MAUSER KAR.98K
SIMILAR TO U.S.M 1903
BOLT OPERATED — MAG.FED
CALIBER 7.92 MM
CLIP 5 RDS — WGT. 9 LBS
RANGE EFFECTIVE 800YDS**

**DUAL PURPOSE M.G.42
REPLACING THE M.G.34
LIGHTER + FASTER RATE OF
FIRE - 1150 R.P.M
SAME CALIBER + FEED BELT
PRODUCED IN MASS
PRODUCTION**

**DUAL-PURPOSE M.G.34
BLOWBACK OPERATED
FAST CHANGING BARREL
CALIBER 7.92MM — BELT 50 RDS
EFFECTIVE RANGE 3800YDS
USED WITH BIPOD OR TRIPOD
AUTOMATIC DEVICE FOR
"SEARCHING FIRE"**

**M.P. 38
MACHINE PISTOL
BLOWBACK OPERATED
MAGAZINE 32 RDS
CALIBER 9 MM
EFFECTIVE RANGE 200YDS**

**M.P. 40
SAME AS THE M.P.38
SLIGHTLY LIGHTER
SLOWER RATE OF FIRE
DESIGNED FOR MASS
PRODUCTION**

A British soldier sights a Bren .303 cal. light machine gun.

An American soldier in Korea sits beside a captured Russian Degtyarov DP 7.62mm. light machine gun.

A Japanese Nambu 6.5mm. light machine gun.

DPM 7.62mm. light machine guns. The basic design for these guns was evolved in the early 1930's and the earlier model, the DP, was field-tested in Spain. The Degtyarovs were exceptionally simple gas-operated guns, fed from pan-type magazines and looking a little like the Lewis guns of World War I. They fired 47 rounds-per-magazine at a rate equivalent to the Bren. The Russians used them in vast quantities as supplements to the standard Tommy guns carried by infantrymen.

The Japanese Nambu 6.5 and 7.7mm. light machine guns resembled the Bren gun but like the Degtyarovs, were far lighter in weight (the smaller calibre Nambu weighed only 19 pounds). Both were commonly used with bayonets fixed to the barrels. They were, in the opinion of many experts, the best Japanese small arms of the war.

TECHNICAL NOTES: The 7.92mm. MG42 Light Machine Gun weighed 25 pounds with bipod, and had a cyclic rate of fire of 900 to 1,200 rounds-per-minute (1,500 r.p.m. on aircraft with certain types of ammunition). The 7.92mm. MG34 weighed 26.5 pounds with bipod, cycled at 800 to 900 r.p.m., and had a maximum range of 5,000 yards. Both guns were fed from 50-round steel belts wrapped in drums. The Bren .303-inch weighed 23 pounds and had an accurate range of 500 yards.

The U. S. Thompson .45 Submachine Gun

THE SUBMACHINE GUN CAME TO PROMINENCE AS A COMBAT WEAPON IN the Second World War. It had the advantage of combining the high volume of fire characteristic of machine guns with the mobility of the rifle. On the other hand, submachine guns were far less accurate than rifles and had a much shorter effective range. Most armies preferred, therefore, to use submachine guns for special purposes—for paratroops, commandos, and the like—and as supplements to, rather than substitutes for, rifles. The great exception to this rule was, of course, the Red Army.

The most famous submachine gun, although not necessarily the most effective, was the American Thompson .45 cal. The weapon gained its reputation before the war as the Tommy gun, the "Chicago piano," of Prohibition days. As adapted for the Army the Thompson was, technically, an excellent gun. "Blowback"-operated, it fired heavy .45 cal. bullets at a rate of about 650 per minute, fed from 50-round drum-type or 20-round box-type magazines. A somewhat similar gun, the Reising, was used by the Marines.

The trouble with the Thompson was that it was too sophisticated to be an ideal combat weapon. It was expensive to produce and its size and complexity sometimes caused field maintenance problems. Both the British and the Americans felt the need for a good submachine gun at least as simple as the German Schmeisser.

The Schmeisser 9mm. MP38 was also a pre-war design, and while not really a simple gun, it was far less complicated than the Thompson.

An American soldier of the 1st Ranger Battalion in North Africa takes aim with a Thompson .45 cal. submachine gun (box-type magazine).

304

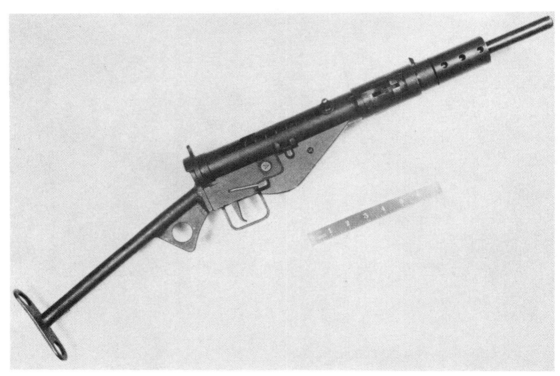

A Russian infantryman fires a PPSH M1941 7.62mm. submachine gun at a low-flying German aircraft.

This British Sten Mk. II 9mm. submachine gun shows the extreme simplicity of construction for which the Sten was famous.

The U. S. M 3 .45 cal. submachine gun was far simpler and cheaper to manufacture than the Thompson.

Constructed for mass production, the MP38 fired standard 9mm. pistol ammunition at a rate of 540 r.p.m. from a 32-round box magazine. It was a light, highly effective weapon and a great favorite with German paratroops and panzer units and, later, with army platoon and section commanders. A later, slightly improved version was known as the MP40. A new and much improved submachine gun known as the MP44 was introduced in the closing months of the war (see picture on page 301).

The Western Allies' answer to the MP38 was the British Sten gun. The Sten was the ultimate in simplicity. It had only 47 parts, most of which were literally stamped from metal like cookies stamped by a cutter. It could be, and was, manufactured by moderately well-equipped underground weapons shops in occupied Europe, and it used the standard German 9mm. ammunition (for the convenience of light-fingered members of the *Maquis*, Home Army, etc.). A similar, ultra-simple submachine gun, the M-3, was subsequently developed by the United States. The M-3, however, continued to use .45 cal. ammunition used by the Thompson, which it largely replaced.

In many respects, Western use of submachine guns was minor in comparison with the massive way the Red Army employed the weapons. The Russians had encountered submachine guns disastrously in the Finnish campaign of 1939–40. Some observers credited the Finnish Suomi gun with inflicting 70 percent of the estimated 250,000 Russian casualties of the Winter War. Be that as it may, the Russians subsequently took up the submachine gun with a vengeance. Their standard weapons were the PPSH M1941 and the PPS M1943, both simple, almost crude guns which fired 7.62mm. ammunition fed from drums or clip magazines. Often used in preference to rifles, the *avtomats* were issued to entire battalions and gave the Russian infantry unequalled short-range fire power.

TECHNICAL NOTES: The Thompson .45 cal. Submachine Gun weighed just under 10 pounds (11 pounds with 20-round magazine), and had an accurate range of 300 yards, a maximum range of 600 yards. The Schmeisser 9mm. MP38 weighed 10.5 pounds with 32-round magazine, cycled at 450 to 550 r.p.m., and had an accurate range of 220 yards. The 9mm. Sten Gun weighed 9.5 pounds with 32-round magazine, cycled at 500 to 550 r.p.m., and had an accurate range of 200 yards.

The U. S. Browning .30 A1 Automatic Rifle

BETWEEN THE SUBMACHINE GUNS AND THE SEMI-AUTOMATIC RIFLES lies a vague category of small arms often described as "automatic." The term doesn't help much since a truly automatic gun *is,* properly speaking, a machine gun. What is usually meant is that groups of rifles and carbines (and the distinction between these is frequently vague enough) which can be fired either automatically or semi-automatically. Unfortunately for the tidy minded, some of the most important World War II weapons belonged to this category.

Of the so-called automatic rifles, the most famous and most widely used was the American Browning .30 cal., better known as the BAR. The BAR was an automatic rifle which could be fired from the shoulder, the hip or, using a bipod mount, from a prone position. The gun could be set to fire automatically at a cyclic rate of either 550 r.p.m. or 350 r.p.m., or it could be set to fire single rounds semi-automatically. A clip containing 20 rounds of regular ball, tracer, armor-piercing, or armor-piercing incendiary bullets was inserted forward of the tigger guard. The gas-operated rifle had a maximum range of about 3,500 yards and an effective range of about 500 yards. In the U. S. Army a few BAR's were normally intermixed with rifles to give small infantry units greater fire power. These versatile weapons proved extremely valuable wherever they were used, especially in the savage jungle fighting on New Guinea and the Pacific islands.

The principal German automatic rifle, the 7.92mm. FG42, was

Aiming from the shoulder, an American soldier in the Philippines fires his Browning .30 cal. Automatic Rifle at a Japanese position.

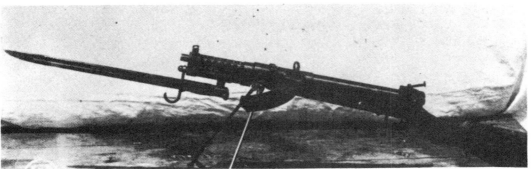

An American G.I. in France holds a captured German FG 42 7.92mm. automatic rifle. A paratroop weapon, the gas-operated FG 42 would cycle at 600 r.p.m.

This Japanese automatic 8mm. paratroop weapon had a hinged stock.

not nearly so widely used as the BAR, nor used like it. It was, nevertheless, a splendid gun and, at ten pounds, weighed far less than the American automatic rifle. Along with Schmeisser 9mm. MP38's, prototypes of the gas-operated FG42 first saw action with the German paratroops who rained down on Crete in 1941.

The best automatic/semi-automatic carbine was the Winchester .30 cal. M2. More than six million of these little five-pound weapons were supplied to American troops, especially to airborne infantrymen, who found the carbine easier to handle than the Garand rifle. The Winchester used both 15- and 30-round clips and was gas-operated. As the war progressed, the Winchester to some extent began to replace the Colt .45 cal. pistol as a standard U. S. side arm.

The Japanese made little use either of submachine guns or "automatic" carbines but towards the end of the war they developed an 8mm. paratroopers' weapon which might be classed in either category. A good, if uninspired gun, it saw very little action.

TECHNICAL NOTES: The Browning .30 cal. A1 Automatic Rifle weighed 17 pounds with 20-round magazine, normally fired 40 to 60 rounds-per-minute at a cyclic rate of 500 r.p.m., and had an accurate range of 600 yards. The 7.92mm. FG42 fired semi-automatic from a closed bolt or automatic lever-selected) at a cyclic rate of 600 r.p.m. from a 20-round magazine. The Winchester .30 cal. M2 carbine weighed slightly over six pounds with 30-round magazine, and had an accurate range of 300 yards, a maximum range of 2,000 yards.

The U. S. Garand .30 M1 Semi-Automatic Rifle

ACCORDING TO GENERAL GEORGE PATTON, THE GARAND .30 CAL. M1 semi-automatic rifle was "the greatest battle implement ever devised." Accepted as the basic U. S. infantry weapon in 1940, the Garand provided the American foot soldier with a rifle unequalled in its combination of accuracy, high rate of fire, and over-all reliability.

Semi-automatic weapons, as a class, were World War II developments. They differed from the standard bolt-action guns in that, as fast as one shot was fired, they automatically cocked the hammer, ejected the spent shell and positioned another. Each shot required a separate squeeze of the trigger, but since that was the only motion required, the semi-automatic's rate of fire could be comparatively high.

A trained rifleman could expend the eight-round clip of an M1 within twenty seconds. He could fire with nearly competition accuracy up to 500 yards and shoot a maximum distance of about 3,500 yards. The gun's magazine could hold regular ball, tracer, armor-piercing or incendiary ammunition; and a relatively simple conversion could turn the rifle into a grenade launcher.

Both the BAR and the Winchester M1 carbine could be fired semi-automatically, but the Garand was superior to the Browning in weight and superior to the carbine in accuracy. And it was, of course, incomparably more accurate than any submachine gun.

The United States was the leading advocate of semi-automatic rifles during the war. The British and the Japanese showed almost no interest

An American infantryman in Germany draws a bead on an enemy sniper. His rifle—probably the most famous of all U. S. weapons —is the Garand .30 cal. M1 semi-automatic.

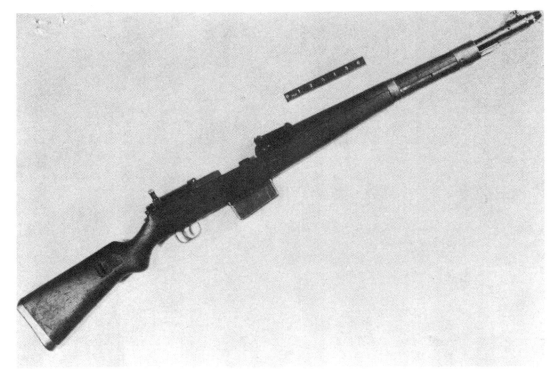

The U. S. Winchester .30 cal. M1 carbine was semi-automatic. The M2 and subsequent versions could also be fired automatically.

The German semi-automatic G-41 7.92mm. rifle was unsatisfactory. A later weapon, the G-43, was better, but was developed too late to see significant service.

in the guns and Russian experiments with the semi-automatic shoulder weapons proved unsuccessful. Early in the war Russia supplied its infantry units with large quantities of the Tokarev M1940 7.62mm. semi-automatic carbine. The gun's design was so defective, however, that it was withdrawn from service and the Red Army finished the war using bolt-action M1891-30 rifles and M1944 carbines.

In view of the fact that the Germans had just about every other kind of weapon, it is not surprising that they should have had a semi-automatic rifle too. They did, and it—the 7.92mm. G41—was a serviceable gun, though much inferior to the Garand. The G41 was operated by gas which was trapped in an odd cone-shaped device fitted on the muzzle and drove a floating piston. The rifle accepted cartridges from two 5-round clips. The G41 did not begin to appear in significant quantities until the middle of the war and never entirely replaced the standard German bolt-action Mauser rifle. Late in the war the Germans introduced a much improved semi-automatic rifle, the G43, but this weapon saw very little action.

TECHNICAL NOTES: The Garand .30 cal. M1 Semi-Automatic Rifle weighed 9.5 pounds and fired from an 8-round clip to a maximum range of 3,500 yards. The 7.92mm. G41 weighed 11 pounds, and using two 5-round Mauser clips fired 10 rounds a maximum range of 1,320 yards.

The British Lee Enfield .303 Bolt-Action Rifle

IN SPITE OF THE PREPONDERANCE OF AUTOMATIC, SEMI-AUTOMATIC, and special weapons used by the troops which fought in World War II, the simple, bolt-action rifle played a crucial role in every army. One of the best was the British Lee Enfield whose basic design dated from the 1890's. A number of versions were produced, of which the S.M.L.E. or .303-inch Short Magazine Lee Enfield was the most widely used. Known officially as Rifle No. 1 Mark III, it armed the "Tommies" that fought on foot in every battle area from Malaya to the Rhineland.

The Mark III was superior to most other bolt-action rifles in many ways, not the least of which were its locking system and easy field maintenance. The former made the Mark III's in particular, and all Lee Enfields in general, the fastest operating bolt-action rifles in the world. Firing from a box-type magazine extending through the bottom of the stock forward of the trigger guard, the Mark III carried a full load of two 5-round clips which a trained soldier could expend with reasonable accuracy in slightly less than a minute. The Mark III, however, was not intended for rapid fire.

The standard bolt-action rifle of the Japanese Army was the Arisaka Model 38, produced in both 6.5mm. and 7.7mm. versions. Comparatively simple in design, the Arisaka 38 had a permanent magazine and used a 5-round clip. It was reliable, but not exceptionally accurate. Its parts were roughly machined by American and British standards, and loose-fitting. The gun rattled. It was not a weapon to carry on night patrol or maneuvers requiring stealth or silence.

British soldiers on parade in Korea carrying Lee Enfield .303 cal. bolt-action rifles. The British Army used several versions of the Lee Enfield during the war, all more-or-less similar.

An American soldier aims a Springfield .30-06 cal. bolt-action rifle.

Russian snipers carrying Moisin M91/30 7.62mm. bolt-action rifles.

The standard German war-time rifle was the Mauser 98K, a somewhat shortened version of the famous old Mauser 98.

The basic bolt-action rifle of the Red Army was the Moisin 7.62mm. M1891-30. Automatic, semi-automatic, and submachine guns eventually supplanted the 91-30 as a primary infantry weapon, but it was undeniably reliable and effective in its sphere, and performed excellent service as a sniper's gun in the hands of both guerrillas and regular troops during some of the worst fighting of the war. A simple modification of the Moisin converted the gun into a bolt-action carbine known as the M1944.

The standard U. S. bolt-action rifle of World War II was the sturdy, dependable Springfield .30-06, which first proved its mettle as an infantry weapon during World War I, when it established a reputation for being the most accurate military rifle ever developed. It had an effective range of 600 yards and an extreme range of 3,300 to 5,500 yards, depending on the type of ammunition used. Though primarily army weapons, Springfields were used with highly satisfying results as sniping rifles by Marines on Guadalcanal during the first major U. S. offensive of the Pacific war. American infantry also used the U. S. Enfield .30 cal. M1917 bolt-action rifle, a modified version of the standard British Lee Enfield chambered to accept the rimless cartridge used by the Springfield.

The standard German bolt-action rifle, the Mauser 7.92mm Gew 98, was a very old and very famous gun. Its bolt-action system was the most widely used in the world and provided the pattern for many later rifles, including the American Springfield. Accurate, reliable, and sturdy, the Mauser was easily modified into both long- and short-barreled carbines. Its operational characteristics were essentially the same as those of the Springfield.

TECHNICAL NOTES: The Lee Enfield .303-inch Bolt-Action Rifle weighed close to nine pounds and fired 10 rounds from two 5-round clips using sights adjustable for 200 to 2,000 yards' range. The Arisaka 6.5mm. Model 38 weighed slightly less than nine pounds and fired from a 5-round clip to an accurate range of 500 yards, a maximum range 4,000 yards. The Springfield .30-06 cal., weighing a little over eight pounds, fired from a 5-round clip, and could penetrate solid wood 15 inches thick at 600 yards.

The German Walther 9mm. 38 Automatic

ADMITTEDLY THE FINEST MILITARY HAND GUN USED IN WORLD WAR II was the German Walther 9mm. 38 automatic. The grip, balance and hang of the P-38, as it was commonly called, were every bit as excellent as the internationally famous Luger, of which it possessed all the good points and eliminated a majority of the bad. Operated by recoil and the only standard military pistol with a double action hammer, the P-38 fired eight rounds from a handle clip and was extremely accurate up to a maximum range of 75 yards. The striking energy of its bullet was exceptionally high. Its reputation for reliable performance and technical perfection made the P-38 a much coveted souvenir among Allied troops.

Doubtless the most famous hand gun in the United States, and one whose name is synonymous with brute force in a small arm, is the Colt .45 cal. automatic pistol. No matter where it hit, the heavy bullet of the Colt .45 could usually stop and disable an enemy. It was carried by officers, squad leaders, and military policemen, and was effectively used on night patrol, and in close hand to-hand and house-to-house combat. It fired eight rounds in rapid sequence fed from a handle clip. More than two million Colts were manufactured and used in World War II. It was standard U. S. Army issue.

As a side arm, the British in World War II relied on the Enfield .380 Pistol No. 2 (revolver). Lighter than the Colt .45, but proven equally effective in combat, the Enfield revolver achieved its end by firing a heavy bullet at a comparatively low velocity. Standard issue for British forces, it was used for close-in fighting.

This 1943 British War Office display of hand guns shows, among others, the German Walther 9mm. 38 (top right), Luger 9mm. 08 (top left) and Mauser 7.63mm. (top center); the Italian Beretta 9mm. 1934 (bottom center); and the British Enfield .38 cal. No. 2 (bottom left.)

The American Colt .45 cal. automatic pistol.

The Japanese Nambu 8mm. automatic pistol.

The standard Japanese service pistol of World War II was the Nambu 8mm. automatic. It resembled the German Luger and was fashioned in such way as to permit the attachment of a stock for use as a carbine. The Nambu 8mm. fired a specially designed cartridge from a handle clip holding seven rounds. It had an accurate range of 75 yards and a maximum range of 1,400 yards. A 7mm. version was reported produced for use by officers. A 9mm. was made for use as a carbine when fitted with a stock.

There were, of course, other famous hand guns used during the war: the British Webley .45 cal. revolver, the American Smith and Wesson .45 cal. revolver, the French Service 8mm. revolver, the German Mauser 7.63mm. automatic, the Italian Beretta 9mm. automatic, the Russian Tokarev 7.62mm. automatic, and many more. Each has its admirers and detractors and all lay claim to the attention of the weapons buff. Unfortunately, space does not permit even brief descriptions of these many fine weapons.

TECHNICAL NOTES: The Walther 9mm. 38 Automatic weighed 34 ounces, was 8.5 inches long overall, had a maximum M.S.E. of 460 f.p. and fired eight rounds an accurate range of 75 yds. The Colt .45 cal. weighed 39 ounces, was 8.5 inches long overall, and fired eight rounds (seven in the clip, one in the chamber) an accurate range of 75 yards and a maximum range of 1,600 yards (achieved by elevating the pistol to 30 degrees). The Enfield .380 Pistol No. 2 weighed 27.5 ounces, was 9.5 inches long overall, and fired six rounds from its cylinder an accurate range of 50 yards, a maximum range of 800 yards.

MISCELLA-NEOUS WEAPONS

MISCELLANEOUS WEAPONS, FOR THE PURPOSE OF THIS BOOK, IS MERELY a catch-all category for types of weapons not mentioned elsewhere. In all frankness, this section might have caught a good deal more than it has. The sole justification for omitting sections on hedge-hogs, depth charges, bombs, aerial rockets and much, much more is, quite simply, lack of space. The authors apologize for this, but in truth, the line has to be drawn somewhere.

That the most important weapons included in this category are the "V" rockets and the atomic bomb goes without saying, but perhaps not enough public attention has been given the significance of still another class of weapons: naval mines, the use of which may yet prove to be the most all-encompassing means of carrying on an offensive against ships. One reason why more has not been written about mines is that, for most of the war, they played a secondary role. The only major mine campaign was undertaken after VE day, at a time when the defeat of Japan was already a foregone conclusion, and its significance was largely overshadowed by the air raids, naval victories and atomic bombings which attended the death throes of the Japanese Empire.

Yet the effects of the great mine offensive against Japan, begun in March, 1945, were impressive. Thousands upon thousands of mines dropped from Twentieth Air Force B-29's so clogged the channels of every important Japanese and Korean seaport that effective minesweeping operations became impossible. This lethal ring of sound, magnetic and pressure mines sank over 670,000 tons of enemy shipping and virtually severed Japan's lifelines to the outside world. It is quite possible that, had it been continued, the mine campaign alone could have starved Japan into defeat. It is interesting and a little frightening to speculate on the relevance of this experience to the future conduct of war.

The German V-1 and V-2

IN JUNE, 1944, THE THREE-SIDED ALLIED VISE OF MEN AND WEAPONS
that cupped Germany on the west, east, and south, began slowly to be
screwed shut. It Italy, Salerno and Anzio were past, as was the five and
a half month long Battle of Cassino. The American Fifth Army was in
Rome, the invasion of southern France impended. The British Eighth
Army, having by-passed the eternal city, was in full cry, driving the
German Tenth Army ever northward. The Second Front had been
opened. American and British troops and tanks were in Normandy and
the Red Army was embarked on the monstrous offensive that was to
take it to Berlin. Hitler's claim that the Allies would never set foot in
his "Fortress Europe" had been refuted. The war was in its final phase,
and the Third Reich had begun its last-ditch stand for survival. It was
from amidst this atmosphere of chaos and ruin that Germany launched
the first of the brilliant, terrible *Vergeltungswaffen*—the weapons of re-
venge, the V-weapons.

Commonly referred to as the "Buzz Bomb" because of the shrill,
sputtering whine it emitted in flight, the V-1 was initially—and for some
time exclusively—launched against London. Beginning on D-day plus 6,
from bases along the French coast in the Pas de Calais sector, great
overhead shoals of the robot bombs whined across the English Channel
to the British capital at approximately 400 m.p.h. on pre-set courses.

More than 8,000 V-1's, each carrying a ton of high explosive which
detonated upon contact, were sent off to London. However, less than

The pulse-jet motor of this V-1 "buzz bomb" has just cut off and
the missile is diving swiftly and silently into the heart of London.

A big German V-2 rocket on its launching pad.

A V-1 on display at Clovis Army Airfield after the war.

half ever reached the sprawling city. Vulnerable to anti-aircraft fire and fighter attack, the V-1 became a prime flak target and the natural prey of fighters such as the swift Hawker Tempest. Upwards of 630 V-1's were exploded by Tempests which met the bombs as they crossed the Channel. Nevertheless, those robots which found their targets took a devastating toll. The stubby-winged, pulsejet-driven bombs killed nearly 6,000 Londoners, injured another 40,000, and damaged or destroyed more than 75,000 homes.

The V-1 was the first of Hitler's *Vergeltungswaffen*; the second, more deadly, more complex in conception, was the V-2 supersonic rocket. Known to its makers as the A-4, it was launched against England mainly from bases in the Low Countries.

The first V-2 hit England on September 8, 1944. Opening the space age, it came hurtling down upon Chiswick at 3,500 m.p.h.—over four times the speed of sound.

Until the Allies destroyed and overran its bases, nothing could deter or nullify the V-2. It could not be seen, heard—or intercepted, for it rose to an altitude of some 60–70 miles. About one thousand V-2's were rained on England. Five hundred hit London and caused nearly 10,000 casualties. Later on, after the V-1 and V-2 bases in France and the Netherlands were destroyed and the Germans pushed out of the Low Countries, both missiles were fired at Allied installations in Liege and Antwerp. They killed 8,000 Belgians and injured more than 23,000.

As a military missile, the V-2 was peerless. It remained unique long after the war ended, and its impact upon the conduct of war and the entire concept of aerial weapons was immense. Originally planned as the forerunner of a long-range missile to be launched against the continental United States, the V-2 subsequently "fathered" the whole first generation of American and Russian space missiles and ICBM's.

TECHNICAL NOTES: The V-2 ballistic rocket missile weighed 13 tons (including a one-ton high-explosive warhead, four tons of liquid fuel—alcohol, and five tons of liquid oxygen to implement combustion), had a reaction engine delivering a 52,000-lb. thrust equal to 600,000 h.p. a top speed of Mach 5 (3,500 m.p.h.), a 225-mile range, 116-mile ceiling, was 46 ft. long and 5.5 ft. in diameter, with a stabilizing finspan of 11.8 ft.

Land and Sea Mines

THE LAND MINE PLAYED ITS MOST PROMINENT COMBAT ROLE IN THE desert campaign. In some ways the most sinister weapon used in North Africa, it claimed countless victims on both sides. It was the treacherous, unseen vanguard that met every advance of troops and armor.

Prior to the third and last Battle of El Alamein, in front of their lines between Tel el Eisa and the edge of the Qattara depression, the Germans put down half a million anti-tank and anti-personnel mines in giant chessboard patterns. As many as one thousand mines a night were set by the sappers of the Panzer Army Afrika who rigged them to explode by means of intricate networks of tripwires as well as by pressure from above. Before the main section of their front great minefields called "Devil's Gardens" were put down according to plans reportedly conceived by Rommel himself, with whom minelaying and mine-detection were arts. In addition to standard German Tellermines, special traps were made up of Italian hand grenades, "T" mines, and 50- and 250-lb. *Luftwaffe* bombs wired to go off at the slightest touch.

Complex-patterned minefields also were a major feature of German defenses at El Agheila following the rout of Rommel's command west from El Alamein in October and November, 1942. The British first became acquainted with the diabolical "S" mine at El Agheila. Set off by trip wires, the "S" mine popped two to six feet up in the air like a jack-in-the-box before exploding and flinging a deluge of shrapnel in all directions as far as 100 yards.

A war-time display of German anti-vehicular and anti-personnel mines and hand-grenades.

GERMAN MINES

MAGNETIC HOLLOW CHARGE
CHARGE 6.6 lbs
USED FOR DISABLING
ARMORED VEHICLES

A.T. TOPF MINE
CHARGE 12.5 lbs
FIRING PRESSURE 570°
CAN NOT BE
DETECTED WITH
MINE DETECTOR

TELLERMINE 35
CHARGE 12 lbs
FIRING PRESSURE 175°
MIGHT FIRE IF
STEPPED ON BY ANY
PERSONNEL

MAGNETIC HOLLOW CHARGE
CHARGE 7.9 lbs
USED FOR DISABLING
ARMORED VEHICLES

TELLERMINE 43
~MUSHROOM~
FIRING PRESSURE 570°
USUALLY BOOBY-
TRAPPED AGAINST
LIFTING

TELLERMINE 42
CHARGE 12 lbs
FIRING PRESSURE 570°
ALL TELLERMINES ARE
USUALLY FOUND
IN PAIRS

MODIFIED SHU-MINE
CHARGE 3 lbs
FIRING PRESSURE 75°
USUALLY THICKLY
SCATTERED IN ANTI-
TANK MINEFIELDS

'S' MINE
~BOUNCING BETTY~
CHARGE 1 1/4 lbs
EXPLODES 3-5 ft ABOVE
THE GROUND
USED EXTENSIVELY
WITH TRIP WIRES

STICK GRENADE MODEL 24
THIS MODEL IS
NOW USED MAINLY
FOR TRAINING

The German Shu mine consisted of a ½-lb. of TNT in a wooden box. The lid was propped partly open with a twig. When the twig was disturbed and the lid snapped shut, the mine exploded.

These German self-propelled mines were remote controlled. Called "Doodle-bugs" by the Allies, they were ineffective and seldom used.

The larger type of the early German magnetic naval mine. This example was recovered in late 1939.

Another special anti-personnel mine used by the Germans was the wooden-case Schu mine, which could not be detected by the electro-magnetic brooms used by Allied sappers. Usually thickly scattered in with anti-tank mines, Schu mines more frequently injured than killed, often blowing off a foot when stepped on. They were used in staggering quantity at Cassino where mines were one of the most devastating features of German defenses, and in the two-mile stretch of mines that confronted American troops when they crossed the upper Rapido.

Naval mines were extensively used by most of the major combatants. German magnetic mines caused considerable damage to Allied shipping until a simple method (called "degaussing") was found to neutralize ships' magnetic fields. Big German defensive mine fields along Channel coast sank a number of Operation Overlord ships and caused the Underwater Demolition Teams severe problems. In the Pacific, mine laying was conducted sporadically by both sides until, at the end of the war, the U. S. undertook a major campaign of aerial mine laying around the Japanese home islands. The campaign was begun in March 1945 and between that time and the end of the war, over 670,000 tons of shipping were sunk and every one of Japan's important seaports was virtually sealed off.

TECHNICAL NOTES: The U. S. M1A1 anti-tank mine was representative of its type. It weighed 10.67 lbs. and contained 5.8 lbs. of TNT. Buried 3″ beneath the surface, it was set to detonate at a pressure of 500 lbs. without the "spider" attachment or of 250 lbs. with the "spider". The conventional British H.2 horned naval mine weighed 650 lbs. and was detonated by light contact.

Torpedoes

LAUNCHED FROM SUBMARINES, ALLIED PT- AND MTB-BOATS, AXIS E-boats, destroyers, and such planes as the American Douglas TBD, British Fairey Swordfish, and Japanese Mitsubishi G4M1, torpedoes sent hundreds of thousands of tons of U. S., English, German, Italian, Japanese, and neutral merchant ships to the bottom, and accounted for a fair number of the naval vessels of both sides given the deep six in battle and caught in ambush in port or enroute to and from the scene of action.

At the outset, the American steam-driven Mark 14 torpedo showed serious defects in its detonating and depth-control systems. An early example of what this could mean in combat was exhibited by the experience of *Sargo* during the Japanese invasion of the Philippines. *Sargo*, in eight separate attacks, fired 13 torpedoes, not one of which exploded on its target. For the first two years of the war, American submariners were obliged to put up with the idiosyncrasies of the Mark 14.

Japan's turbine-driven torpedoes, in contrast, functioned well. Their 24-inch "Long Lance" surpassed the 21-inch Mark 14 in deadliness and range. But despite their technological advantage, the Japanese failed to make torpedoes a major submarine weapon.

By 1943 American Mark 18 electric torpedoes, copied from captured German models, had been brought up to adequate performance standards and the Navy turned the weapons on Japanese shipping with devastating effect. American submarines are credited with sinking 63 percent of Japan's merchant fleet and a smaller, but very impressive, percentage of her warships.

A famous photograph taken through the periscope of an American submarine shows a Japanese warship which has just fallen victim to U. S. torpedoes.

This batch of German electric torpedoes on a flat-car in captured Bremen never got to sea.

A German aerial torpedo in a re-inforced case.

Despite the early effectiveness of her undersea campaign, Germany too was at first beset with torpedo troubles. But the German solution to these difficulties was considerably better than adequate. The first innovation was the smooth-running wakeless electric torpedo which could be set to travel either a straight or a zigzag course. Then came the deadly *Zaunkönig,* an acoustic torpedo which homed on the cavitations of ships' propellers. Fortunately for the Allies, the Germans had only begun to explore the potentialities of the acoustic torpedo when the war ended.

Aerial torpedoes did not differ in principle from other varieties, but they were sometimes slightly modified in form in an attempt to avoid such problems as plunging, porpoising and premature detonation which inevitably accompanied launchings from a high fast-moving platform.

TECHNICAL NOTES: The U. S. steam-driven Mk. 14 torpedo had a speed of 32-46 knots (depending on range) and a 668-lb. warhead. The electric Mk. 18 had a top speed of 29 knots and a 670-lb. warhead. The electric Mk. 20 had a top speed of 40 knots and a 1,000-lb. warhead.

Grenades and Flamethrowers

TWO CLASSES OF SMALL, PORTABLE WEAPONS ADDED IMMEASURABLY TO the armament and fighting abilities of the individual Allied and Axis soldier during World War II: the grenade and the flamethrower.

The grenade is perhaps the simplest hand weapon ever devised for doing extensive damage. Basically, it is a small, fused bomb which explodes whether it hits its target or not. Once the firing pin is pulled, nothing can deactivate a grenade. Hundreds of thousands of "pineapples" and "potato mashers" were manufactured and used by both sides. They were either thrown—their effective range depending on the heaving ability of the user—or launched from standard army rifles easily fitted with special accessories in the field. Special grenade launchers were also developed and used. In general, these operated much like the Very pistol and used a shell-type grenade which detonated upon contact. One such launcher, used by the Russians, projected a .66 pound grenade up to 800 meters.

American troops used three types of grenade in close combat: the "pineapple" with an iron body scored so it would break into fragments, for defense; a can-shaped grenade with a cardboard body containing a powerful charge, for offense; and a phosphorous grenade for laying down a fog-like screen to conceal small troop movements. The well-known "potato masher" high-explosive grenade was the typical German weapon. The Russians also used "potato mashers" with cloth streamers attached to stabilize the weapons in flight.

An American G.I. in France inspects a German static (i.e., nonportable) flamethrower. The device could be used defensively or offensively (when mobilized on an armored vehicle.)

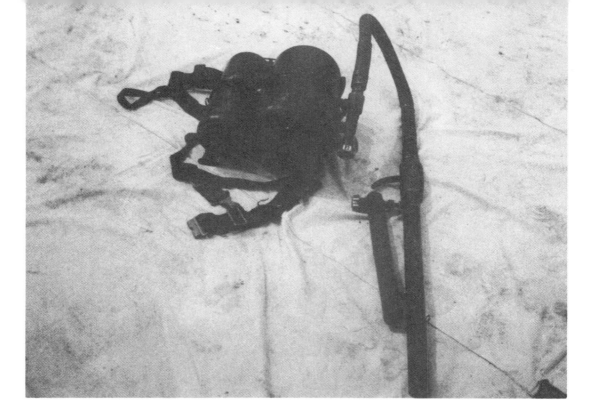

This German portable flamethrower captured in Italy looked much like standard Allied weapons.

The simplest kind of hand grenade is the homely "Molotov cocktail": A bottle of gasoline to which is attached either a wick or a detonator. This example was captured by U. S. forces in Italy.

Despite their small size, grenades proved extremely valuable in offense against pillboxes, gun emplacements, machine gun nests, and other small concentrations of enemy troops. Circumstances also made it possible for Allied and Axis infantrymen alike to knock out tanks with grenades.

Unquestionably the most effective weapon for its purpose, and the most dramatic and terrifying of the war, was the flamethrower. It was most used by the American troops against the Japanese in the Pacific island strongholds—particularly on Iwo Jima, and against the Russians by the Germans who found the weapon indispensable for routing the Red Army out of dugout positions.

The flamethrower was simplicity itself. It consisted of a fuel tank of mixed gasoline and oil, a pressure tank, and a hose with an adjustable nozzle for controlling the length and extent of the stream of flame it shot.

While basically a one-man weapon, the flamethrower was also used mounted on tanks. The Americans, the Germans and the British used flamethrowing tanks in the concluding battles of the war in Europe. Russia also motorized flamethrowers. Special large versions of the weapon fired short bursts up to 150 yards.

Flamethrowers were highly effective against tanks, pillboxes, and similar small heavily armored and fortified targets. It is said that human beings caught directly in the blast of a flame thrower were killed instantly. One hopes this was so.

TECHNICAL NOTES: The U. S. Fragmentary Grenade weighed approximately 16 ounces and consisted of three basic parts: the body, fuse, and explosive charge. The U. S. Flamethrower, filled, weighed upwards of 60 pounds, the gun weighing around eight pounds, was roughly 2.5 ft. long and fired a burst of eight or nine seconds duration better than 20 yards.

The Atomic Bomb

ON THE WARM, SUNNY MORNING OF AUGUST 6, 1945, THE CONDUCT OF war was irrevocably changed for all time by a cataclysmic roar in the quiet, cloudless sky above the sprawling Japanese city of Hiroshima on the delta of the Ota River. The titanic force and result of the explosion dwarfed every aspect of the intense, bitter conflict it was to end. Announced by a glaring pink-white glow and followed by a tremendous wave of suffocating heat and wind, the blast ushered the world and its inhabitants into a new age: the atomic.

That morning, four B-29 Superfortresses suddenly appeared above the just-awakened metropolis. Among them was the B-29-45-MO (44-86292), the "Enola Gay," piloted by Lt. Colonel Paul W. Tibbetts, Jr., and named in honor of his mother. The giant plane had lifted history off the runway of the airfield on Tinian, south of Saipan in the Mariana Islands, at 2:45 A.M. For six and a half hours it had flown to meet the dawn with its companions, leisurely and unopposed. Over Hiroshima, two of the four planes turned and droned away south toward Okinawa where the United States was massing a gigantic force for the invasion of the Japanese mainland. The "Enola Gay" and the fourth plane circled the city, then departed toward the Bingo Sea at high speed.

As the "Enola Gay" approached the Japanese coast its bomb-bay doors swung open slowly. On the instrument panel in front of the pilot the altimeter registered 31,600 feet. Ground speed was calculated to be 328 m.p.h., slightly less than the maximum attainable at that height. At

The mushroom cloud over Hiroshima which brought an end to the most mechanized and terrible war in history.

The Hiroshima bomb was called "Little Boy." It weighed 9,700 lbs. and had the explosive power of 20,000 tons of TNT.

"Fat Man," the Nagasaki bomb, was a 20-kiloton weapon in which the U-235 charge was imploded to critical mass by an outer shell of small explosive charges.

0915 Major T. W. Ferebee, the bombardier, activated the bomb release. From the belly of the plane a long, dark, cylindrical-shaped object plummeted downward, its spiral flight checked by a small parachute. Nicknamed the "Little Boy," the cylinder weighed 9,700 pounds. It was 129 inches long and 31.5 inches in diameter. Four antennae in its tail vibrated in the faint south wind that blew as it fell toward the heart of Hiroshima. Inside were 137.3 pounds of Uranium 235, divided in two masses.

When the strange, rocket-like object came within 800 feet of the city, a charge of powder sent one Uranium mass into the other through a hollow tube. Nuclear fission began one fifteen-hundredth of a microsecond later. The detonation which followed laid waste to 4.7 square miles of Hiroshima. It killed 78,150 and injured 37,425 persons out of a total population of 343,969. Another 13,083 were reported as missing. The "Enola Gay" returned to its base. Behind it mushroomed the mark of its success—a sun-eclipsing cloud which soon reached a height of forty thousand feet.

The next day, the President of the United States announced: "Sixteen hours ago, an American airplane dropped one bomb on Hiroshima. That single bomb had more power than twenty thousand tons of explosive. It is an atomic bomb."

While the President spoke, Tokyo radio issued a call to capitulate: "Hiroshima . . . dead too numerous to count . . . honorable peace . . . new weapon and flames from the sky . . . honorable peace . . . honorable peace."

TECHNICAL NOTES: Other than the statistics of total weight, length, girth, method of controlled descent, weight of nuclear explosive and type employed, mentioned in the above text, no technical data on the first atomic bomb used in war has been disclosed for general circulation.

Grateful acknowledgment is made to the United States Department of Defense, the United States Army, the United States Navy, the United States Air Force and the Ordnance Museum at Aberdeen Proving Grounds for permission to use all photographs used in this book with the following exceptions: The Imperial War Museum, London, pages 97, 146 (bottom), 169, 206 (middle); SovFoto, pages 214 (middle and bottom), 233, 234 (middle), 273, 274 (bottom); Wide World Photos, pages 82 (bottom), 117, 345; Black Star, page 98 (bottom).

20 °K